THE
PRIVATE-
LANGUAGE
PROBLEM

ATE DUE

STUDIES

IN PHILOSOPHY

Consulting Editor:

V. C. CHAPPELL,
The University of Chicago

THE PRIVATE-LANGUAGE PROBLEM

A Philosophical Dialogue

by John Turk Saunders

and Donald F. Henze

both of San Fernando Valley State College

RANDOM HOUSE   NEW YORK

ACKNOWLEDGMENTS

We wish to thank the publishers concerned for granting permission to quote from the following works: A. J. Ayer, *Language, Truth and Logic* (London: Victor Gollancz Ltd., 1936; 2nd edn., 1946); *Individuals:* P. F. Strawson, Methuen & Co. Ltd. (London); R. Descartes, *Meditations on First Philosophy*, in *Philosophical Writings*, trans. and ed. by G. E. M. Anscombe and P. T. Geach (London and Edinburgh: Thomas Nelson & Sons Limited, 1954); R. Carnap, *The Unity of Science*, Psyche Miniatures, General Series No. 63, trans. by M. Black (London: Kegan Paul, Trench, Trubner, and Co. Ltd., 1934); L. Wittgenstein, *Tractatus Logico-Philosophicus*, trans. by D. F. Pears and B. F. McGuinness (London: Routledge and Kegan Paul Ltd., 1961). Quotations from *Philosophical Investigations* by permission of the Executors of Ludwig Wittgenstein and Basil Blackwell, Oxford. Sydney Shoemaker, *Self-Knowledge and Self-Identity*. Copyright 1963, Cornell University. Used by permission of Cornell University Press; Norman Malcolm, *Knowledge and Certainty: Essays and Lectures*, © 1963. Reprinted by permission of Prentice-Hall, Inc., Englewood Cliffs, N.J.

TO VALERIE

TO INGRID AND
CHRISTOPHER

PREFACE

The idea for this book grew out of departmental discussions of Wittgenstein's *Philosophical Investigations* during 1961 and 1962. From that time to the completion of the book, one of us believed a private language to be impossible, and the other held the opposite view. Neither knew how the book would end. Consequently, it was natural for us to fall into the use of dialogue form; this mode of exposition contributed greatly to the objectivity and the excitement of our enterprise. We tried to do our best for both sides of the debate, letting chips fall where they may. Like spectators, we awaited the outcome of the developing dialogue. To our surprise (and relief), we found at the book's end that we had been led neither to continue to disagree nor to compromise, but rather to agree thoroughly upon our conclusions, conclusions the specific content of which neither of us had anticipated.

We gratefully acknowledge assistance from the San Fernando Valley State College Foundation in the form of two grants during 1963–64 and 1964–65 that enabled us to obtain secretarial help in preparing the typescript of this book. We wish to express our appreciation to Mr. Roy Holland, who read and criticized an earlier version of Chapter I; to Professors Charles Chastain, Keith Donnellan, and Douglas Long, who read and commented upon the finished manuscript; to Mrs. Dorothy Johnson and Mrs. LuAnne Rohrer for their countless and often unerring secretarial assists; to Mrs. Marion Kost for her splendid typing; and to Valerie Neill Saunders for secretarial aid and for preparing the author index. We are indebted to all those who responded so promptly and generously to our requests for reprints of published articles and copies of unpublished papers. Finally, we wish to thank our colleagues in the philosophy department at San Fernando Valley State College for the helpful and stimulating discussions on private language that they have shared with us.

Regarding our footnote references to articles: When articles have appeared in more than one place, the page references in our footnotes refer to the first place cited in any given bibliographic listing.

J.T.S.

D.F.H.

September, 1967

CONTENTS

THE
PRIVATE-
LANGUAGE
PROBLEM

I |
The Nature of the Private-Language Problem

1) The Historical Setting of the Problem

The idea of a private language has, in a way, a long history: Opinions that entail the possibility of a private language—whether or not their advocates were aware of this logical commitment—can be traced back to Hobbes and Descartes, and perhaps as remote a figure as Protagoras would have to be included in a historical survey of the subject. Locke, for instance, had a theory about words and their meanings that made out public languages to be somehow derived from numerous private languages, but he did not put it in these terms. In another way, the idea of a private language is a twentieth-century phenomenon: for it is primarily in the twentieth century that questions regarding the nature and possibility of a private language have received explicit formulation and specific attention. It may, therefore, be said that this nest of questions, which constitutes the private-language problem, is at once as old as philosophy and as new as television.

If one attends to those beliefs that entail the existence of a private language, it is possible to discern in the writings of many important philosophers certain jobs that such languages were to perform. They were to function as the bases upon which public languages and shared knowledge develop; and/or they were to serve as means of self-communication, enabling the user to think either in terms of a private vocabulary with its private meanings or to think by means of the private meanings of words that also have a common meaning in virtue of being part of a public vocabulary.

Contemporary interest in the possibility of a private language has been stimulated mostly by some passages in Wittgenstein's *Philosophical Investigations* (hereafter abbreviated "*Inv.*").[1] Prior to the publication of *Inv.*, explicit references were made to private language both by Wittgenstein himself and by other philosophers such as Schlick and Ayer.[2] Nevertheless, Wittgenstein is the pivotal figure, and his treatment of private language in *Inv.* is a natural point of departure.

---

[1] Trans. G. E. M. Anscombe (Oxford: Basil Blackwell, 1953). Passages in Part I are referred to by section number alone, e.g., "177"; passages in Part II are referred to by page number, e.g., "p. 177."

[2] Cf. L. Wittgenstein, *The Brown Book* (Oxford: Basil Blackwell, 1958), p. 105 (cf. these implicit references in *The Blue Book* [Oxford: Basil Blackwell, 1958], pp. 60, 65, 72–3); M. Schlick, "On the Relation Between Psychological and Physical Concepts," in H. Feigl and W. Sellars, eds., *Readings in Philosophical Analysis*, W. Sellars, trans. (New York: Appleton-Century-Crofts, Inc., 1949), pp. 405–6 (at any rate, "private language" was employed by Schlick's translator); A. J. Ayer, *The Foundations of Empirical Knowledge* (London: Macmillan and Co. Ltd., 1940), Sec. 13.

2) The Meanings of "Private Language"

The sort of private language that Wittgenstein wishes to attack is characterized in *Inv.*, 243, and there, too, it is carefully distinguished from other kinds of private language that he finds unobjectionable. We separate three portions of this section in order to make these distinctions more apparent:

(i) . . . we could imagine human beings who spoke only in monologue; who accompanied their activities by talking to themselves.—An explorer who watched them and listened to their talk might succeed in translating their language into ours.[3]

(ii) But could we also imagine a language in which a person could write down or give vocal expression to his inner experiences—his feelings, moods, and the rest—for his private uses?—Well, can't we do so in our ordinary language?

(iii) But that is not what I mean. The individual words of this language are to refer to what can only be known to the person speaking; to his immediate private sensations. So another person cannot understand the language.

It is evident from (i) and (ii) that Wittgenstein allows that there can be private uses for language,[4] for exam-

[3] Compare the supposition, evidently rejected, in *Inv.*, 344: "Would it be imaginable that people should never speak an audible language, but should still say things to themselves in the imagination?" Cf. also *Inv.*, 347–49.

[4] This is more apparent if it is realized that the crucial phrase in the German text of (ii), *"für den eigenen Gebrauch,"* may be translated alternatively as "for his own/special/peculiar use."

ple, talking to oneself, keeping personal diaries, or devising secret codes (or secret languages). But soliloquies may be overheard and understood or, in the more extreme case of (i), may be comprehended and eventually translated by one who takes note of the correlation between monologic utterances and activities. Diaries may be unlocked and read by persons other than their authors. They may even be published and may come to reach a wide audience. Codes can be broken and secret languages deciphered. In short, when words are put to such private uses, then what is now personal or secret may conceivably come to be publicized or disclosed. We shall refer to such languages as *factually* private languages since their privacy is a contingent matter of fact that could have been otherwise: it is not a conceptual truth that such languages be private. It is this sense of "private language" that is closest to the *ordinary* uses of the phrase.

On the other hand, (iii) depicts the sort of language that Wittgenstein wishes to repudiate. It is languages that are more or less on the order of (iii) that have been characterized as "private languages" in *philosophical* usage. We use the phrase "more or less" because several different concepts of private language are relevant here.[5] We distinguish some of them as follows:

(PL$_1$) A language, each word of which refers to experiential data, although each of these words is conceptually independent of publicly observable phe-

---

[5] It has come to our attention that our PL$_1$-PL$_2$ distinction is somewhat similar to B. Medlin's distinction between "private$_1$ language" and "private$_2$ language" in his "Critical Notice" of A. J. Ayer's *The Concept of a Person and Other Essays*, *Australasian Journal of Philosophy*, XLII (Dec., 1964), 414-15.

nomena.[6] (When we say that an experiential-datum term, "E," is *conceptually independent* of publicly observable phenomena, we mean this: The existence of an E neither entails nor is entailed by the existence of any publicly observable phenomena; nor is it part of the meaning of "E" that publicly observable phenomena provide evidence for the existence of an E.)

(PL₁′) A PL₁ that one learns from one's own case by associating linguistic terms with one's own experiential data.[7]

(PL₂) A language that only the speaker/user (logically) can understand.

These are all kinds of language whose privacy, in one way or another, is not merely a contingent matter of fact: a PL₁ is so defined that its terms are logically (conceptually) independent of publicly observable phenomena, and a PL₂ is defined as a language that it is logically impossible that more than one person understand. We shall refer to such languages as *logically* private languages, since it is a conceptual truth that they possess the sorts of privacy that they do. It is logically private languages that Wittgenstein impugns and with which the private-language problem is essentially concerned: hence,

---

[6] Cf., e.g., *Inv.*, 206–7, 243, 256–57, 360, 580, p. 178 (penultimate par.). Malcolm remarks in N. Malcolm, "Wittgenstein's *Philosophical Investigations*," *Knowledge and Certainty: Essays and Lectures* (Englewood Cliffs, N.J.: Prentice-Hall, Inc., 1963), p. 97: "At bottom it [the idea of a private language] is the idea that there is only a contingent and not an *essential* connection between a sensation and its outward expression."

[7] Cf., e.g., *Inv.*, 258, 293, 295, 347.

throughout this book "private language" (hereafter abbreviated "PL") will mean *logically* private language, unless otherwise specified, and, in general, "private" will mean *logically* private.

By refining (iii) in the foregoing way, we hope not only to achieve increased clarity but to avoid begging the question at the outset against those of Wittgenstein's opponents who maintain that a PL_1 is not necessarily a PL_2.[8] For the present, it remains an open question whether the terms of a PL_1, which are private in the aforementioned respect, are also private in the sense that one who speaks a PL_1 can know about and talk about only his own experiential data, not those of another person. We present PL_1' as a species of PL_1 in light of the possibility that one possess a language without having learned it: one may, for example, be born with such knowledge, or one may acquire it by means of drugs or a brain operation.[9]

It is important to note that a PL_1 is not to be equated with a sensation language, that is, a language to be characterized by the definition of "PL_1," only replacing "experiential data" by "sensations." The P-L problem is concerned with all kinds of experience, and the language and knowledge thereof, not just sensations such as pains,

---

[8] We are not sure if Wittgenstein would maintain the equivalence of PL_1 and PL_2. But it is clear that many of his opponents, viz., those who accept the analogy argument regarding other minds, would repudiate this thesis. We therefore separately define "PL_1" and "PL_2" and leave to further discussion the important issue as to whether or not a PL_1 is necessarily a PL_2. It is interesting to note that J. J. Thomson in "Private Languages," *American Philosophical Quarterly*, I (Jan., 1964), 29–30, offers a recipe for constructing PL_2's that are not PL_1's.

[9] Cf. P. T. Geach, *Mental Acts: Their Content and Their Objects* (London: Routledge and Kegan Paul, 1957), p. 19; and Malcolm, *op. cit.*, p. 112.

tickles, and feelings of warmth. Wittgenstein often chooses sensation talk by way of example, but a perusal of *Inv.* renders it incontestable that his interest in the P-L problem was not confined to its bearing upon sensation languages. We use the term "experiential data" to cover not only experiences themselves—sensations, emotional feelings, and thoughts—but also any alleged objects of "direct" experience, such as sense data.

It is also true that the P-L problem is concerned not only with experiential data but with all sorts of mental phenomena, such as beliefs, attitudes, moods, intentions, and mental abilities. Thus, "PL₁" might have been still more broadly defined: we might have employed in its definition the term "psychological states" in place of the term "experiential data." We did not do this because it will simplify matters to conduct our investigation of PL by confining our attention, for the most part, to a PL of experiential data. If it should turn out that this sort of PL is possible, this would bode well for the idea that more comprehensive PL's are possible—although the latter would still remain to be proved. If, on the other hand, it should turn out that this sort of PL is impossible, there would remain little hope that a PL of moods, and so forth, is possible.

It is important to see that one who is said to speak a PL₁ may or may not be said to have at his disposal, in addition to the PL₁, some other language or linguistic apparatus. Thus, he may be said not only to speak a PL₁ but also to have the use of physical-object terms such as "arm" and "cloud," and syntactical terms such as "is," "not," "if," and "all." Phenomenalists and dualists alike, for example, are often prepared to claim that they possess the use of both physical-object and syntactical terms, as well as the use of a PL₁. (Of course, it must be recognized that for some philosophers, notably phenomenal-

ists, physical-object terms are reducible to PL_1 terms, and
that a few philosophers have taken syntactical terms to
refer to experiential data such as "no-feelings" and "if-
feelings,"—as Locke seems to have done.[10]) He who op-
poses PL, prototypically Wittgenstein, wishes to oppose
the idea of any and every PL_1, whether the PL_1 be said
to be the only language of a speaker, or whether the
PL_1 be said to be just one of the linguistic resources
possessed by a speaker.[11] It is the unserviceability, indeed the impossibility, of a PL_1, under any conditions
whatever, that is advocated by the Wittgensteinian.
Therefore, in the course of this book, we shall often
deal with the case of a man who is supposed both to
speak a PL_1 and to have other linguistic resources, such
as the use of physical-object terms or syntactical terms,
as well; although we shall always suppose that all of the

[10] J. Locke, *An Essay Concerning Human Understanding*, A. C.
Fraser, ed., 2 vols. (New York: Dover, 1959), Bk. III, Ch. 7,
Sec. 1; cf. Berkeley, *Philosophical Commentaries*, in *Works*
(Edinburgh: Nelson, 1948, 1949), Vol. I, 667. Cf. *Inv.*, pp. 181–
82. In contrast to the Lockean view of syntactical terms, Russell once maintained the possibility of a language whose descriptive terms refer to experiential data and possess only
private meaning, but whose syntactical terms, which do not
so refer, are the publicly meaningful terms of the calculus of
Principia Mathematica. Cf. B. Russell, *The Philosophy of
Logical Atomism*, in R. C. Marsh, ed., *Logic and Knowledge:
Essays, 1901–1950* (London: George Allen and Unwin, 1956), p.
198.

[11] For example, although Wittgenstein sometimes confines his
attention to the case of a man who, apparently, is engaged in
speaking *only* a PL_1 (cf. *Inv.*, 243, 256, 258), he also strives to
establish the specious character of the problem of other
minds: he is here concerned to demonstrate, with regard to
the case of a person who is supposed to speak not only a
PL_1 but also a language in which one can refer to human
bodies and other physical objects of one's environment, that
such a person will not be able to understand talk about the
mental states of others (or oneself). Cf., e.g., *Inv.*, 246, 283–
84, 295–96, 300, 302, 304–8, 390–93, 398, 420, 504, p. 223.

experiential-datum terms that are used by such a person are words in PL_1. In this way, we hope to do some justice both to the variety of proponents of the idea of a PL_1 and also to the Wittgensteinian who wishes to maintain that in no circumstances would such a language be either serviceable or possible.

3) The Nature and Importance of the P-L Problem

The P-L problem may be viewed as a request for an analysis of the different concepts of PL and for a verdict regarding the possibility and/or serviceability of the various kinds of PL. But why, it may well be asked, should such a request be made? By way of reply, we shall now proceed to expand upon our account of the problem and to place it in the philosophical context that gives it importance.

Another way of viewing the P-L problem is to raise it in what Carnap has called the "material mode": Are the data of experience private in the sense that they are conceptually independent of anything that someone other than their "owner" might experience? Could there be minds without bodies? Or, as we prefer to put it, are there (could there be) *private objects*, namely, experiential data that are logically independent of publicly observable phenomena? As Castañeda and Chappell have suggested, it is the private object that Wittgenstein seeks to destroy in his attack upon PL.[12] Chappell may

---

[12] Cf. H-N. Castañeda, "The Private-Language Argument," in C. D. Rollins, ed., *Knowledge and Experience* (Pittsburgh: University of Pittsburgh Press, 1964), pp. 89–91; V. C. Chappell, "Comments" on Castañeda, "The Private-Language Ar-

mislead, however, when he says that Wittgenstein ". . . is not trying to show something about language but rather about sensations or mental phenomena. Linguistic considerations are the means, but an understanding of the latter is the end." [13] For it is the same problem that we raise in the material mode in this paragraph and, in what we call the "formal mode," [14] in the preceding paragraph. To suggest otherwise, in the manner of Chappell, is to run the risk of commitment to the untenable position that Wittgenstein's purposes are extra-linguistic and empirical. In fact, the P-L problem is not a scientific but a philosophical or conceptual matter. The question of the possibility and/or serviceability of the private object is identical with the question of the possibility and/or serviceability of a PL_1. It is this question that constitutes the P-L problem.

Thus, the P-L problem may be said to have its locus in the private object, or, alternatively speaking, in PL_1. As indicated in an earlier footnote, we are uncertain whether or not Wittgenstein would maintain the equivalence of PL_1 and PL_2. It is clear, however, that the concept of a PL_2 plays a crucial role in the attack upon the private object. The arguments with which Wittgenstein and his successors assault the concept of a PL_1 utilize as an important premise the contention that a PL_1 is necessarily a PL_2. This premise they employ as

gument," in C. D. Rollins, ed., *Knowledge and Experience* (Pittsburgh: University of Pittsburgh Press, 1964), p. 118.
[13] Chappell, *op. cit.*, p. 118.
[14] Our distinction between the *formal* and the *material* modes of speech parallels that of Carnap, who introduced these terms, only in part. Thus, we might instead have spoken of *linguistic* and *nonlinguistic* modes of speech. Cf. R. Carnap, *The Unity of Science*, M. Black, trans., Psyche Miniatures, General Series No. 63 (London: Kegan Paul, Trench, Trubner, and Co. Ltd., 1934), pp. 37–42.

a lever with which to topple the idea of a PL_1, maintaining that a PL_2, and thus (given the premise) a PL_1, is not only unserviceable[15] but also impossible. The controversy surrounding this premise remains to be explored.

Why should the private object have caused such a stir? No one, least of all Wittgenstein, would deny the plausibility of the idea of a PL_1. To get a feel for the importance of this issue, and its controversial character, we must turn to some of the perennial epistemological and metaphysical problems of philosophy that constitute its matrix.

3a) PERCEPTION AND THE PHYSICAL WORLD

It may well be true that nobody really doubts the existence of a physical world—a world of rocks, pencils, gases, and animals (including human bodies). But for centuries, philosophers have wondered not only about the ultimate nature of these things but whether genuine knowledge of them is possible and, if so, how it is possible. A perfectly natural point of view to adopt is one that begins at home: Do *I* know of these things? If *I* do, how do I know? Take the most familiar of objects, this coffee cup before me, for example. It is opaque, so I do not now see its back side. But if there is no back side, it is

---

[15] We use the terms "serviceable" and "unserviceable" in a rather technical sense to be elucidated in Sec. 3d and Sec. 4 of Ch. I, and to receive further discussion later on. Roughly speaking, the question whether a PL_1 is serviceable is the question whether it is a possible base for a common language and shared knowledge. Wittgenstein and his successors maintain that a PL_1 is unserviceable in that it is a PL_2. Cf. e.g., Malcolm, "Wittgenstein's *Philosophical Investigations*," *op. cit.*, p. 125: "Private language cannot be the understructure of the language we all understand."

not a cup. Indeed, I do not see a bit beneath the surface of this opaque object. At best my vision takes in its near and outermost surface. But if the matter of the cup does not continue beneath the cup's apparent surface, then the colored expanse that confronts me is not even the near surface of a cup: there is no cup here.

I look again; I feel; apparently, at least, I clink a spoon against the side of the cup. I keep exercising my perceptual attention upon the cup in every way I can think of. But it occurs to me that in each perceptual situation, I am at most presented with one sight, one feel, one sound—never do my senses assure me that a cup is really here before me. At most, I continue to accumulate a variety of cuplike sights, feels, and sounds, a congeries of cuplike experiential data—call them "appearances," or "sense data," if you will. The epistemological problem that confronts me, then, is: What justification can I possibly have for my conviction that there is a cup here? If all that I directly inspect are sense data, how can they support my belief in the presence of a cup?

So runs this ancient and influential approach to a philosophical understanding of perception and the physical world. This brief sketch epitomizes the initial stages of what we shall call the *egocentric outlook* as it applies to the epistemological problems of perception. We now proceed to look at other manifestations of the egocentric outlook in philosophy.

3b) THE NATURE OF THE SELF

Even if it should turn out that I cannot know of the existence of the physical world, how could my convictions regarding my own existence and the nature of myself ever be undermined? It appears that the skeptical doubts that have been raised regarding my perception of the environment in which I seem to find myself could never apply to my knowledge of myself. Those doubts arose because I found that I experience "directly" only sense data (and other experiential data), never physical objects. But surely I cannot be mistaken in thinking I exist, said Descartes. Surely I directly experience myself, and about this may be assured, averred Berkeley.

Nevertheless, this narrow and seemingly secure bastion of genuine knowledge has not been impervious to the subtle infiltration of skeptical doubts. It remained for Hume to note:

> For my part, when I enter most intimately into what I call *myself*, I always stumble on some particular perception or other, of heat or cold, light or shade, love or hatred, pain or pleasure. I never can catch *myself* at any time without a perception, and never can observe anything but the perception.[16]

Where Descartes and Berkeley had found the existence of their selves as simple substances to be self-evident, Hume could not discover such a substance, and the matter was thrown into doubt anew. And when no substance could be produced to endow the evanescent data of experience with unity, the disintegration of any would-be "owner" of these data appeared imminent. Having attempted, by means of memory and the association of ideas, to relate such fragmentary data to one another, Hume was at last compelled to confess that ". . . all the nice and subtle questions concerning personal identity can never possibly be decided . . .";[17]

[16] D. Hume, *A Treatise of Human Nature*, L. A. Selby-Bigge, ed. (Oxford: Clarendon Press, 1888), p. 252.
[17] *Ibid.*, p. 262.

". . . all my hopes vanish, when I come to explain the principles, that unite our successive perceptions in our thought or consciousness." [18]

When the egocentric viewpoint is applied to the self, not only does this problem as to the nature of the self arise, but we must also face the questions: How can I justify my conviction that I can recognize a sensation as a pain, or a sense datum as being blue? How can I know that I am correct when I reason? Perhaps my memory deceives me so that what yesterday I called "tickles" today I call "pains," and what yesterday I called "green" today I call "blue," and so forth. Perhaps I only think I have calculated correctly, although again and again I check the line of my reasoning. What, I wonder, can save me from mistake on these matters? Further, how am I to understand the nature of beliefs, dreams, moods, intentions, attitudes, and purposes? The idea that such states must somehow be explainable simply in terms of experiential data is inviting, yet the task before me seems overwhelming—especially when I am reminded that I am to view these as mental states that are cut off from any conceptual dependence upon physical bodies.

3c) OTHER SELVES

Even if I can somehow find warrant for my conviction that I am an enduring self that has a body among other physical bodies, a self whose perceptions and reasonings are to be trusted, how am I to know that I am not the only conscious occupant of this world in which I find myself? From the egocentric point of view, I must jus-

[18] *Ibid.*, pp. 635–36.

tify my conviction that I live in a society of persons like myself with whom I communicate.

It is only my own thoughts and feelings that I can experience directly, no one else's. Even given that there are bodies like mine that behave like mine, how am I to know that they are animated by minds like mine? Presumably, I must base my belief in the existence of those other persons upon the one thing about them that it is open to me to experience: their behavior. But if I am aware only of their behavior, then perhaps there is nothing behind it. May I not be the victim of a cruel hoax, the lone sentient creature in an otherwise spiritless universe, one man among mockingly lifelike machines?

3d) RESPONSES TO THE EGOCENTRIC PREDICAMENT

The series of problems sketched in Sections 3a–3c may be said to constitute the *egocentric predicament:* the predicament of one who begins "from his own case" and attempts to analyze and justify his system of beliefs and attitudes. This is the predicament of "how to get out," how to move justifiably from one's own experiential data to the existence of an external world containing both animate and inanimate entities. Indeed, as we saw in Section 3b, it is also the problem of "how to get outside" of the experiential data of the present moment, how to warrant one's convictions regarding one's own history and propensities.

If the egocentric predicament be taken as a legitimate problem, then the response to this problem will constitute one or another of the strands composing what we have called the egocentric outlook. This is the outlook of one who begins at home, with the private object (with his own private experiential data), and attempts, in one way or another, to "go abroad." Typical exponents of the egocentric viewpoint are the solipsist, the subjective idealist (Berkeley), the dualist (Locke or Descartes), and the phenomenalist (Russell or Ayer in their early careers). If, on the other hand, the egocentric predicament be viewed as an illegitimate problem, a pseudo-problem, then the response to this "problem" will be to repudiate the egocentric viewpoint. This is the response of one who "begins abroad," who begins in the public rather than the private domain, and attempts in one way or another to understand both of these domains. It is the response of one who holds that only via public standards of justification can our system of beliefs be warranted and understood. This sort of philosopher turns away from PL_1, rejects the private object, in his effort to accomplish the latter task. Typical exponents of the *nonegocentric outlook* are the reductionistic behaviorist, for example, the physicalist (the early Carnap), and the nonreductionistic behaviorist (the later Wittgenstein).

To sum up, a major question in philosophy has always been: How can we justify our beliefs regarding ourselves and the world in which we live? No one doubts that it is through his own personal experience that an individual comes to understand what words mean and comes to know about himself and his world. How else but through his own personal experience could this be done? Certainly the nonegocentric philosopher does not wish to deny this. Where, then, lies the difference between him and the egocentric philosopher? It lies in their approaches to this problem. The egocentric philosopher views the problem in the form of the egocentric predicament, and his response to the problem is one or another egocentric outlook. He begins with what he takes to be the secure "hard data" consisting of private objects, and, taking seriously the sort of skeptical doubts we have rehearsed, he attempts to cope with the difficulties they raise. It is these difficulties that constitute the egocentric predicament, and it is this predicament or problem that he endeavors to solve. The nonegocentric philosopher, on the other hand, refuses to regard the traditional epistemological question as issuing in the egocentric predicament. He begins with what he takes to be the secure "hard data" consisting of publicly observable phenomena, and he usually maintains the essential incoherence of both the notion of the private object and the skeptical doubts to which it leads. The egocentric predicament is seen as being not a problem to be solved but a pseudo-problem to be dissolved. For the nonegocentric philosopher, the genuine epistemological problem is the task of clarifying those public standards of justification that we all employ in science and in everyday life. Wittgenstein, for example, remarks: "What has to be accepted, the given, is—so one could say—*forms of life*" (*Inv.*, p. 226).

Thus, the dispute between the egocentric and the nonegocentric philosophers comes to a dispute over the fundamental nature of justification and, consequently, knowledge. Roughly speaking, the egocentric philosophers hold that the only possible basis for knowledge of anything is the private object, whereas the nonegocentric philosophers hold that the only possible basis for knowledge of anything is the publicly observable object. Hence, the attack upon the private object, upon PL_1, is of the first importance for philosophy. As the P-L problem goes, so goes the status of justification and knowledge. This being so, there is no problem in the theory of knowledge whose fate does not in large part hang upon the disposition of the P-L problem. Having considered, in a general way, the philosophical importance of the P-L problem, we shall now take a closer look at the various responses to the egocentric predicament in order to note the relations in which they stand to the P-L problem. (The relevance of the P-L issue to the philosophical analysis of psychological concepts ought by now to be apparent, and the following material should indicate its relevance to the ancient metaphysical question: What is the ultimate nature of the universe?)

First, the solipsist. One may be a *dogmatic* solipsist, maintaining that nothing exists except himself, his psychological states, and his own experiential data. Or one may take the position of the *agnostic* solipsist: that it is logically impossible that he know of the existence of anything but himself, his psychological states, and his own experiential data. We take our solipsists (among other things) to deny, respectively, the existence of, or knowledge of, any physical objects whatever. Henceforth, we shall use the term "solipsist" to refer to the agnostic solipsist, unless otherwise stated. Thus, the response of the solipsist to the egocentric predicament is to maintain that every attempt to "go abroad," to move from his knowledge of himself and his experiential data to knowledge of something outside this realm, must fail. The solipsist, then, maintains that a PL_1 is possible, for he claims to think in the terms of such a language. But he also holds that a PL_1 is necessarily a PL_2. For it is his position that it is logically impossible for him to know anything about any other persons, and, hence, that even if there were other persons, they would be in the same position with respect to him and could know nothing of him or his language.

Second, we shall place the subjective idealist, the dualist, and the phenomenalist in the same broad category and refer to such exponents of the egocentric outlook as *traditionists*. The subjective idealist insists that the universe is mental throughout, consisting of nothing but minds and their states. The phenomenalist takes the position that the universe is entirely composed of experiential data, some phenomenalists maintaining that these data are neither mental nor physical in themselves (neutral monism), other phenomenalists claiming that they are fundamentally mental. Despite their differences, subjective idealists and phenomenalists alike deny the existence of neither mind nor matter. At most, they adopt a reductionistic view of these categories, maintaining that minds or physical objects are logical constructions out of experiential data so that any statements containing mental or physical terms are completely translatable by statements not containing such terms but containing experiential-datum terms. The dualist holds that the universe contains both mind and matter, and that these are nonreducible or basic categories. What is common to all three of these major types of traditionist viewpoint is the position that philosophy begins "at home," that the private object constitutes the very foundation of our knowledge of anything whatever. Thus, they are committed to the possibility of a PL_1. This position they share with that other egocentric theory, solipsism, but they depart from solipsism in rejecting the notion that a PL_1 is necessarily a PL_2. The traditionists insist that we can and do know of the existence of the world of science and common sense in which there are sticks and stones and other people with whom we live and communicate —and that the basis of our shared knowledge and our common language is the private object, the PL_1. It is because of the popularity and influence of traditionism in the history of philosophy that we shall concentrate upon it to the exclusion of solipsism.

Third, and last, we look at the positions of the behaviorists with respect to the P-L problem. We may distinguish two kinds of reductionistic behaviorism. The *metaphysical* (reductionistic) behaviorist contends that the universe is entirely composed of matter. He does not deny the existence of mind, however, but holds that mental affairs are logical constructions out of physical affairs, notably behavior, so that any statements containing mental terms (or, for that matter, any experiential-datum terms) are completely translatable by statements not containing such terms, but containing physical terms. He therefore flatly denies the possibility of a PL_1. In contrast, the *methodological* (reductionistic) behaviorist (the early Carnap[19]) allows the possibility of a PL_1, although he is convinced that a PL_1 is necessarily a PL_2. He therefore adopts the reductionism of the metaphysical behaviorist, but only for the special purpose of analyzing the intersubjective language of science or daily life: thus he allows that individuals might each possess a language that is both a PL_1 and a PL_2 and that is, therefore, distinct from the intersubjective language of any community. The latter kind of language, in his view, must always be a language in which mental affairs are logical constructions out of physical affairs.

Like the reductionistic behaviorist, the nonreductionistic behaviorist does not deny, but affirms, the existence of mental affairs; but unlike him, the nonreductionistic behaviorist does not maintain that mental affairs are logical constructions out of physical affairs. He emphatically denies the possibility of the requisite translations but equally emphatically insists that this should not be taken to imply that there remains a mentalistic residue that is logically independent of publicly observable

---

[19] *Op. cit.*, pp. 60–65, 76–93. That Carnap would have granted the possibility of a PL_1 is here at least suggested, although not explicitly asserted. For the expression of a similar position, cf. Schlick, *op. cit.*

phenomena. He is no less opposed to the private object than is his metaphysical counterpart: for the nonreductionistic behaviorist, a PL_1 is impossible; the notion of the private object is an incoherent notion; any significance that psychological terms may possess lies in their connections with publicly observable phenomena. As indicated early in Section 3, this sort of philosopher also contends that a PL_1 is necessarily a PL_2, and this contention plays an important role in his endeavors to establish the impossibility of a PL_1. Even if he should fall short of the latter goal, however, there is, as we shall see, reason to believe that the nonreductionistic behaviorist would cling to his contention and maintain on this basis that a PL_1, if not impossible, is at least *unserviceable:* that is, that it is not, *contra* the traditionist, a possible base for a common language and shared knowledge.[20]

Obviously, we have in mind Wittgenstein and his successors as the exemplars of nonreductionistic behaviorism. It is therefore worth adding that Wittgenstein took great pains to make clear that he does not deny the existence of mental affairs and that he is not a reductionistic behaviorist.[21] Yet we, too, have made it clear that these positions are incompatible with the viewpoint of the nonreductionistic behaviorist. Obviously, then, we do not attribute them to Wittgenstein. Would Wittgenstein be willing to accept for himself the label "nonreductionistic behaviorist"? We doubt it. But then philosophers of his style are prone to shun labels. Would his successors— Malcolm, Strawson, or Shoemaker, for example—willingly receive this appellation? Again, we doubt it. The term

[20] Cf. Ch. III. For example, it is clearly Malcolm's view (cf. Malcolm, "Knowledge of Other Minds," *Knowledge and Certainty, op. cit.*), that one who speaks a PL_1 could not so much as speak meaningfully about the mind of another.

[21] Cf. e.g., *Inv.*, 183, 244, 304–8, 486, pp. 179–80, p. 220.

"behaviorist" bears a curiously odious aroma in philosophy these days and is therefore unlikely to be welcomed by those to whom it is applied. Admittedly, too, we ought to be wary of placing Wittgenstein and all of his various successors in one basket. Nevertheless, needing a convenient label for the opponent of PL_1, the foe of the private object, we shall call him the *Wittgensteinian*. And although we use this title rather than any title involving "behaviorist," it is only candid to note that our Wittgensteinian is precisely the sort of man we had in mind in depicting what we have called the "nonreductionistic behaviorist."

4) Prospectus

Having discussed the nature and importance of the P-L problem, we ought now to give some indication of our plans for investigating this matter in what follows. We shall consider the defense of the private object from the point of view of the traditionist, and it is the Wittgensteinian whom we cast in the role of its assailant.[22] (Not many would wish to emulate either the solipsist or the reductionistic behaviorist.) If the traditionist is correct, not only is a PL_1 possible, but it is the base of our common language and our shared knowledge, and, hence, a PL_1 is not necessarily a PL_2. If, on the other hand, the

[22] There is great diversity amongst the views held by those who tend to be Wittgensteinians and also amongst the views of the philosophers who tend to be traditionists. The traditionist and the Wittgensteinian of our book are ideal types: we are sure that there is no one philosopher who would subscribe to all of the positions taken by our traditionist or by our Wittgensteinian.

Wittgensteinian is correct, then a PL_1 is impossible; and, further, even if it were possible, it would not be *serviceable*, that is, it could not be the base for a common language and shared knowledge, since a PL_1 is necessarily a PL_2.

Clearly, then, the major questions to be considered are these:

(1) Is a PL_1 impossible?
(2) Is a PL_1 necessarily a PL_2?

Complete victory for the Wittgensteinian would consist in his establishment of an affirmative answer to both (1) and (2). Complete victory for the traditionist would consist in his establishment of a negative answer to both (1) and (2).[23] The only clear-cut alternative is that of partial victory and partial defeat for each side, which would consist of a negative response to (1) and an affirmative response to (2).

Although we shall examine the P-L problem against the background of the controversy between traditionism and Wittgensteinianism, it is worth noting here the bearing upon the other epistemological positions, previously delineated, of the possible results of this study. The solipsist's position with respect to minds (or persons) will have been vindicated if the Wittgensteinian is wrong about (1) but right about (2). Thus, Wittgenstein concurs with the solipsist in thinking that a rigorous development of the notion of the private object leads in-

---

[23] Such a victory, we take it, involves proof that a PL_1 is serviceable, but not that it is, in fact, the base of our common language and our shared knowledge. The latter contention of the traditionist's shall be considered only to the extent that it is involved in the question of the serviceability of a PL_1: beyond this, the matter shall be left to some future battle.

exorably to a solipsism with respect to other minds. They are joined in this position by the methodological behaviorist, who shares with the solipsist, as against both the Wittgensteinian and the metaphysical behaviorist, the view that a PL_1 is possible.

The assaults upon PL_1 may be divided into two kinds, an *internal* attack and an *external* attack.[24] The internal attack, which we might appropriately have named the "strong" or "devastating" attack, is designed to show the impossibility of a PL_1. The arguments leveled against the possibility of a PL_1 all employ as a premise an affirmative answer to (2). We shall therefore view the internal attack as a two-pronged assault. The first prong is an attempt to establish a Yes answer to the following:

(3) Given that a PL_1 is necessarily a PL_2, is a PL_1 impossible?

The second prong is an attempt to establish a Yes answer to (2). The external attack, which we might appropriately have named the "weak" or "crippling" attack, is calculated to show that a PL_1 is unserviceable. On our usage of *serviceable*, a PL_1 is unserviceable if, and only if, the answer to (2) is affirmative,[25] and therefore the external assault consists in an attempt to establish a Yes answer to (2). Hence, the external attack is the second prong of the internal attack. Nevertheless, it is of interest independent of its role in the internal attack, for should the first prong of the latter fail while the second

---

[24] Cf. Malcolm, "Wittgenstein's *Philosophical Investigations*," *op. cit.*, p. 105.
[25] To put this in the material mode: On our usage of *serviceable*, private objects are unserviceable if and only if no one (logically) can know of the private objects of another. Additional senses of "serviceable" will be introduced and discussed in Ch. IV.

succeeds, then the internal attack will have failed although the external attack will have succeeded. By this measure, then, may the comparative merits of Wittgensteinianism and traditionism be gauged.

We shall begin, in Chapter II, with the first prong of the internal attack and examine a number of arguments that the Wittgensteinian marshals in behalf of a Yes answer to (3). In Chapter III we shall turn our attention to the external attack (the second prong of the internal attack), the Wittgensteinian's arguments for a Yes answer to (2). Chapter IV is devoted to a bevy of issues arising out of the ascription argument, a Wittgensteinian onslaught upon the private object involving both prongs of the internal attack. In Chapter V, we shall offer an assessment of the results of our investigation.

II |
The Internal Attack: Prong One

1) Prologue

We shall now examine the first prong of the internal attack. For this purpose, it will be assumed that the private object is unserviceable, that is, that a PL_1 is necessarily a language that no one other than its speaker (logically) can understand. Thus, the question before us is: Given that a PL_1 is necessarily a PL_2, is a PL_1 impossible?

Of course, a traditionist would not grant the truth of the assumption. He maintains that a PL_1 is the language that enables him not only to commune with himself but also to communicate with others, that it is the basis of our common language and shared knowledge. Nevertheless, the traditionist holds that, as such a basis, it is a language that he might speak whether or not he could speak it with others. It is his contention that it is because he can speak such a language that he is able to communicate with other persons. He therefore comes under fire when the Wittgensteinian launches the first prong of the internal attack, and he is obliged to defend against this assault. The traditionist's battle against the proposition that constitutes this assumption, the proposition that a PL_1 is necessarily a PL_2, will come under study in Chapters III and IV. In the present chapter, we have to consider whether it is possible for one to speak a PL_1, even given that this is a language that he could not share with anyone else.

The background of the debate that is to occupy us in the present chapter may be viewed in this way: There have been philosophers of the highest reputation who, in looking for a sound beginning for their philosophizing, unhesitatingly proceeded on the belief that one *must* begin with one's own private experiential data (cf. Ch. I, Sec. 3). These "hard data" are the source of one's knowledge, one's concepts, one's language. A traditionist philosopher might depict this situation as follows:

> Feelings, sensations, and thoughts are a fair sample of what is given to me. What could be more intimately connected to me? And what could be more certain than the fact that I feel, or sense, or think something? Descartes was surely right when he wrote: ". . . it is I who have sensations, or who perceive corporeal objects as it were by the senses. Thus, I am now seeing light, hearing a noise, feeling heat. These objects are unreal, for I am asleep; but at least I seem to see, to hear, to be warmed. This cannot be unreal; and this is what is properly called my sensation. . . ." [1]
>
> These primitive, immediate, incorrigible elements of my experience are plainly the model referents of a

---

[1] R. Descartes, *Meditations on First Philosophy*, in R. Descartes, *Philosophical Writings*, E. Anscombe and P. T. Geach, trans. (Edinburgh: Nelson, 1954), *Med.* II, p. 71.

language, my language. I not only have such experiences, but I know that I have them: I think about or reflect upon them. The language I employ for these purposes is a PL₁, a language whose words refer to private objects. Witness, again, Descartes: "I will now shut my eyes, stop my ears, withdraw all my senses; I will even blot out the images of corporeal objects from my consciousness; or at least (since that is barely possible) I will ignore them as vain illusions. I will discourse with myself alone and look more deeply into myself; I will try to grow by degrees better acquainted and more familiar with myself." [2]

So I commune with myself. I mull over private objects. I am aware of a sequence of experiential data. Indeed, I am aware of *different* experiential data. And being able to discriminate readily among them—picking them out—I can assign names to them that capture their differences and similarities.

So says the traditionist. Clearly, it is incumbent upon him to beat off any assault upon the integrity of the alleged language in which he speaks (or thinks) of his own private objects: he must endeavor to refute the Wittgensteinian charge that his putative language is not only unintelligible to others but also unintelligible to himself. A traditionist would certainly wish to maintain not only that a PL₁ is serviceable, but also that, whether or not it is possible for other persons to understand his PL₁, he himself can surely speak such a language. He would insist that he can know about and think about his own private experiential data quite independently of the question of whether he can know of the data of others or they can know of his experiential data. Thus, the traditionist will urge the denial of the Wittgen-

<hr>

[2] *Ibid., Med.* III, p. 76.

steinian contention: given that a PL_1 is necessarily a PL_2, a PL_1 is impossible.

2) *Idle Ceremony*

One of the defining features of a PL_1 is that its terms refer to experiential data. But, asks Wittgenstein:

> How do words *refer* to sensations? . . . how is the connection between the name and the thing set up? . . . how does a human being learn the meaning of the names of sensations? (*Inv.*, 244)

A traditionist may naturally respond by saying that he can give himself a kind of ostensive definition. Wittgenstein argues, however, that this so-called definition must remain but an *idle ceremony*.[3]

Wittgenstein imagines the traditionist developing his case by supposing that he wants to keep a diary of certain sensations he has:

> Let us imagine the following case. I want to keep a diary about the recurrence of a certain sensation. To this end I associate it with the sign "E" and write this sign in a calendar for every day on which I have the sensation. I will remark first of all that a definition of the sign cannot be formulated.—But still I can give myself a kind of ostensive definition.—How? Can I

[3] Cf. R. Rhees, "Can There Be a Private Language?" *Proceedings of the Aristotelian Society*, Suppl. XXVIII (1954), 77, 80–81; A. J. Ayer, "Can There Be a Private Language?" *The Concept of a Person and Other Essays* (London: Macmillan and Co. Ltd., 1963), p. 42.

point to the sensation? Not in the ordinary sense. But I speak, or write the sign down, and at the same time I concentrate my attention on the sensation—and so, as it were, point to it inwardly. (*Inv.*, 258) [4]

Wittgenstein thinks that this accomplishes exactly nothing, that it is but an idle ceremony. The foregoing passage continues:

But what is this ceremony for? for that is all it seems to be! A definition surely serves to establish the meaning of a sign.—Well, that is done precisely by the concentrating of my attention; for in this way I impress on myself the connexion between the sign and the sensation.—But "I impress it on myself" can only mean: this process brings it about that I remember the connexion *right* in the future. But in the present case I have no criterion of correctness. One would like to say: whatever is going to seem right to me is right. And that only means that here we can't talk about "right."

There is at least one thing here concerning which Wittgenstein is indisputably correct: that the meaningfulness of a sign can in no way be guaranteed by any ritual performance in which one attends to some phenomenon and, as it were, pledges to use the sign to refer to this and similar items. It is, indeed, tempting to suppose that such a ceremony will suffice to endow a sign with meaning, but in the *Philosophical Investigations* Wittgenstein returns again and again to this topic, and he has there revealed the ludicrous falsity of this supposition. There is a treacherous allure to the idea that a

[4] Should it be thought that the diary-keeper is a straw man of Wittgenstein's invention, compare Locke's version of the private recorder, J. Locke, *An Essay Concerning Human Understanding*, A. C. Fraser, ed. (New York: Dover Publications, Inc., 1959), Bk. III, Ch. 9, Sec. 2, with *Inv.*, 256–63.

sign's having meaning for a person is something that can take place all in a flash,

> . . . something mental: he as it were takes it [the meaning] into his own mind. If he then does something further with it as well, that is no part of the immediate purpose of language.[5]

Yet Wittgenstein has once for all exposed the mistaken

> . . . conception of naming as, so to speak, an occult process. Naming appears as a *queer* connexion of a word with an object.—And you really get such a queer connexion when the philosopher tries to bring out *the* relation between name and thing by staring at an object in front of him and repeating a name or even the word "this" innumerable times. For philosophical problems arise when language *goes on holiday*. And *here* we may indeed fancy naming to be some remarkable act of mind, as it were a baptism of an object. (*Inv.*, 38)

At this point we may imagine the traditionist engaging the Wittgensteinian in the following dialogue:

T: "*This* point of Wittgenstein's I am quite prepared to grant. Of course, he is correct when he says:

> . . . naming is a preparation for description. Naming is so far not a move in the language-game—any more than putting a piece in its place on the board is a move in chess. We may say: *nothing* has so far been done, when a thing has been named. It has not even *got* a name except in the language-game. (*Inv.*, 49)

He is within his rights to ridicule those traditionists who speak 'As if what we did next were given with the mere

---

[5] *Inv.*, 363. Cf., e.g., *Inv.*, 20, 73, 132, 149, 191, 197, 262–63, 268, 274, 311, 362, 414, 454, 507, 692–93.

act of naming' (*Inv.*, 27). This much Wittgenstein has taught us, and we are grateful. Certainly, my private ostensive definition is not a success unless I proceed to act in accordance with it. But it is my contention that I can do precisely this, that I can keep my diary and in so doing adhere to the rule that I am to apply 'E' to those and only those experiential data that are of the same kind as the datum to which I attend in ostensively defining 'E.' (Indeed, as Wittgenstein indicates, a special ceremony is not necessary if I am meaningfully to use my terms: what is essential is that I use them consistently, that is, in accordance with a rule or standard.) I therefore part company from Wittgenstein when he says that I cannot tell whether or not I am using 'E' correctly, that is, in accordance with this rule. I remember perfectly well how I have used 'E': I remember that I have been using 'E' correctly."

W: "You fail to heed Wittgenstein's warning that

> . . . to *think* one is obeying a rule is not to obey a rule. Hence it is not possible to obey a rule 'privately': otherwise thinking one was obeying a rule would be the same thing as obeying it.[6]

> Are the rules of the private language *impressions* of rules?—The balance on which impressions are weighed is not the *impression* of a balance.[7]

You think that it is enough to say that you can remember that you have followed the rule by using 'E' in a certain way. But it is essential to the concept of memory that a memory impression (memory belief) may be mistaken. What reason do you have to think that in the

[6] *Inv.*, 202. Cf. *Inv.*, 269, 380.
[7] *Inv.*, 259.

past you have used 'E' in accordance with the rule? You are under the impression that this is what you have done. You have memory impressions of having done so. *As you remember it,* this is what happened. But this is the only reason you can have, since you claim to speak a PL₁. And if this putative reason is your only possible reason, then you can have no reason at all for thinking that you have followed a rule. For a memory impression may be correct or incorrect, and you have no possible way of knowing which of these characterizes your memory impressions. Indeed, you do not even have memory impressions of private sensations: a memory impression is something that can be found to be correct or incorrect, unlike these supposed memory impressions (cf. *Inv.,* 51). Will you say, 'Well, I *believe* that this is the sensation again'? Wittgenstein's sarcasm is apt: 'Perhaps you *believe* that you believe it!' (*Inv.,* 260). At best you can only believe that you believe it, since you cannot have so much as a memory impression regarding your past sensations."

T: "Wittgenstein enjoins us: 'Imagine someone saying: "But I know how tall I am!" and laying his hand on top of his head to prove it' (*Inv.,* 279). You wish to say that my method of determining the history of my sensations is as idle as this method of determining one's height. You would have it that my memory impressions (memory beliefs) in no way justify me in thinking that I have used 'E' in a certain way. You therefore contend that I speak no PL₁, follow no linguistic rules, have no notion of 'correct' and 'incorrect,' and, indeed, have no memory beliefs concerning my private sensations. But your reason for saying that my so-called memory impressions provide me with no reason for thinking that I have followed a rule is simply that nothing else could justify me in thinking this. It seems natural for me to conclude that you are merely denying the legitimacy of reliance upon memory as a mode of justification. Surely it is absurd to assert that I cannot trust my memory. Yet if you renounce this absurdity you must admit that it is proper for me to trust my memory. And if this is proper, then I do after all have reason to believe that I have kept my diary in accordance with my rule for 'E,' and hence that I speak a language, a PL_1, in which I meaningfully employ the sign 'E.' " [8]

3) Checking Up on One's Memory Impressions

W: "Your conclusion is mistaken: it is no part of my position to repudiate the trustworthiness, the cognitive authority, of memory beliefs (memory impressions).[9] We do have the epistemic right to trust our memories, but only if a certain condition is satisfied. Indeed, it is the satisfaction of this condition that is essential to one's so much as having a concept of memory—to one's having memory beliefs (impressions). And it is this very condition that is absent from your supposed language. This condition is that it be possible to check up on our memory impressions in order to find out whether they are veridical or not.

"As Wittgenstein indicates, we must be prepared to answer the question:

[8] Cf. C. Wellman, "Wittgenstein and the Egocentric Predicament," *Mind*, LXV (April, 1959), 225; C. Wellman, "Wittgenstein's Conception of a Criterion," *Philosophical Review*, LXXI (Oct., 1962), 444–47.
[9] Cf. *Inv.*, 53, 56; Rhees, *op. cit.*, 83.

But what do we regard as the criterion for remembering it right? . . . Imagine that you were supposed to paint a particular colour 'C,' which was the colour that appeared when the chemical substances X and Y combined.—Suppose that the colour struck you as brighter on one day than on another; would you not sometimes say: "I must be wrong, the colour is certainly the same as yesterday"? This shews that we do not always resort to what memory tells us as the verdict of the highest court of appeal.[10]

When you wonder about the meaningfulness of the sign 'E' that you write in your diary, you have but one course open to you, to consult your memory. At best, you have only your own memory impressions with which to attest your claim that you have written 'E' when you have had a certain private sensation. Clearly, you are committed to accept your own memory as 'the highest court of appeal.' It is for this reason, and not because there is something the matter with memory as such, that it is not open to you to rely upon your memory in the matter before us. Your apparent memory could not be tested for correctness, and hence is not even memory. The thesis that you speak a PL_1 could not be tested for truth, and hence is not even a thesis. Your apparent language is not a language."

T: "But why do you say that I have only my own memory impressions with which to attest my claim that I have written 'E' when I have had a certain private sensation? This may or may not be so, just as it may or may not be so that I have only my own memory impressions with which to attest my claim that I have written 'M' when there was a tree before me. If I have kept a

[10] *Inv.,* 56. Cf. *Inv.,* 51, 53.

motion-picture camera running and focused upon me and my environment, then I shall have its pictures with which to check upon my memory belief that I have said 'M' when there was a tree before me. If neither a camera nor anything else that might be put to this use has been available to me, then I shall not have anything with which to check upon my memory belief. Similarly, if I have kept running and attached to me a machine that records my physiological condition (blood pressure, etc.), then I shall have its recordings with which to check upon my memory belief that I have said 'E' when I had a certain sensation. If neither such a machine nor anything else that might be put to this use has been available to me, then I shall not have anything with which to check upon my memory belief.

"I would agree with you when you say that it is essential to the concept of memory that it be possible to check upon our memory impressions in order to find out whether or not they are veridical. Hence, I am willing to admit that I could not be said to use my memory in the case at hand and so could not be said to speak a PL_1 if it were impossible for me to check upon my memory impression that I have used 'E' in a certain way. I would agree with Malcolm and Wittgenstein about the sense-lessness of the claim that one *might* be right in using 'E,' that it could happen that one is following a rule, *even if* there is no possible way of checking on this.[11] I contend, however, that it is possible for me to employ such checks not only when I think that I have used a sign in association with physical objects such as trees but also when I think that I have used a sign in association with private experiential data such as my sensations."

[11] Cf. N. Malcolm, "Wittgenstein's *Philosophical Investigations*," *Knowledge and Certainty: Essays and Lectures* (Englewood Cliffs, N.J.: Prentice-Hall, Inc., 1963), pp. 99–100.

W: "You rightly see that it is the logical possibility, not the de facto accessibility, of checks upon one's memory beliefs that is requisite to the concept of memory. Photographs may or may not have been taken, and, in general, checks upon one's memory belief may or may not happen to be available. If they are not, this in no way impugns the idea, or possibility, of such a memory belief. One does not cease to have a memory belief as soon as any evidence that might serve as a check upon the veracity of that belief disappears (e.g., when films or fingerprints are destroyed in a fire). It is, as you say, the (logical) possibility of such checks that is essential.

"But you quite fail to see that there are no possible checks upon your putative memory impression of having had certain private sensations. You think that the machine you suggest will provide such checks. But what reason is there to suppose that the charts produced by such a machine have any relevance to private sensations? It is not open to you to treat it as a *conceptual* truth that these charts, or behavior, or any other publicly observable phenomena, constitute evidence for the occurrence of sensations. For to do so is to abandon the thesis that these are *private* sensations, *private* objects, items that are conceptually independent of publicly observable phenomena. To do so is not only to allow that your sensation language is not a PL_1 but also to allow that it is not a PL_2: for if it is a priori true that publicly observable phenomena count as evidence for the occurrence of your sensations, then it would be possible for persons other than yourself to understand your sensation language. You must therefore treat it as an *empirical* truth that there is a correlation between such charts and such sensations in virtue of which these charts constitute evidence for the occurrence of your sensations. And what empirical reason can you have to believe that there is such a correlation? Presumably, you shall appeal to your memory impression that when in the past sensations of this kind occurred, the charts were also forthcoming. But this is to beg the question: it is to respond to the charge that there are no possible checks upon your memory impression of having had certain sensations by appealing to your memory impression of having had these very sensations or other sensations of the same kind. What is in question is the possibility of your checking upon your memory impression of having had certain sensations of a specific kind. To appeal to another memory impression of having had these same sensations or certain other sensations of the same kind will not help to provide you with a check. If the first impression can be checked only by means of another impression of the same kind, then neither of them can be checked at all. It is as if you were to tell me that the way to check upon one's impression that something is an X is to find out whether the thing to its left is an X. If this is the only possible check upon one's impression that something is an X, then there are no possible checks upon such an impression."

T: "As you say, for me it is not a conceptual truth that publicly observable phenomena, such as charts or behavior, count as evidence for the occurrence of sensations: this would, indeed, violate my conception of experiential data as being private. But I deny that I am in the position of one who can tell whether something is an X only by determining whether the thing to its left is an X. It is true that I must *empirically* establish the evidential value of the charts that I employ in order to check upon my memory impression that I have written 'E' in my diary when, and only when, I have had a certain kind of sensation. You wrongly assume, however, that to do so I must appeal to my memory impression(s) that when in the past sensations of this kind occurred, the charts were also forthcoming. I may also have found that sensations of other kinds were regularly correlated with charts (i.e., chart-readings) of other kinds, so that it is probable that the original charts were also correlated with sensations of the kind I claim to call 'E.' I may also have found that the original charts were regularly correlated with condition C, for example, a pin's being stuck into my unanesthetized arm, and, in addition, that C's have been regularly correlated with sensations of the kind to which I claim to refer with 'E.' Further, I may *now*, again and again, stick a pin into my unanesthetized arm and find each time that the sensation thereby produced is of the same kind as the sensations that I claim to have called 'E,' and so forth. I would therefore maintain that I can, without begging it, answer the question whether my initial memory impression is correct, for I can, in answer, appeal to other memory impressions that are not of the same kind as the one in question."

W: "Oh, you may appeal to different memory impressions all right, and even memory impressions of different kinds, if you like. But in every case, your alleged answer to the question whether your initial memory impression is correct is an answer that rests essentially upon an appeal to some memory impression of yours, a memory impression to the effect that one or another group of sensations has been correlated with something or other. Each of these memory impressions is an impression of the past occurrence of sensations. Yet it is the possibility of checking upon your memory impressions regarding the occurrence of sensations that is in question. Hence, you cannot establish this possibility by appeal to any of your own memory impressions of sensations. Since it is impossible for you to check upon your memory impressions of sensations in a way that does not involve appeal to other of your memory impressions of sensations, it is impossible for you to check upon your memory impressions of sensations in a way that does not appeal to other of your own memory impressions. But if you can check your own impressions only by means of your own impressions, you cannot check your own impressions at all. The following comments of Wittgenstein's apply:

> Let us imagine a table (something like a dictionary) that exists only in our imagination. A dictionary can be used to justify the translation of a word X into a word Y. But are we also to call it a justification if such a table is to be looked up only in the imagination?— 'Well, yes; then it is a subjective justification.'—But justification consists in appealing to something independent.—'But surely I can appeal from one memory to another. For example, I don't know if I have remembered the time of departure of a train right and to check it I call to mind how a page of the time-table looked. Isn't it the same here?'—No; for this process has got to produce a memory which is actually *correct*. If the mental image of the time-table could not itself be *tested* for correctness, how could it confirm the correctness of the first memory? (As if someone were to buy several copies of the morning paper to assure himself that what it said was true.)
>
> Looking up a table in the imagination is no more looking up a table than the image of the result of an imagined experiment is the result of an experiment." (*Inv.*, 265)

T: "Previously I accused you of holding the absurdly skeptical view that we haven't the epistemic right to trust our memories, and you denied the charge. You said that you demanded only that it be possible to check upon our memory impressions (or memory beliefs), and I agreed with the legitimacy of this demand. But when I tell you my way of checking upon my memory impressions with regard to my PL_1, for example, my use of 'E' in my private diary, you refuse to allow that the checks that I propose are really checks. And why do you say that they are not checks? Because they involve appeal to memory impressions of mine that cannot themselves be checked upon in any way that does not involve further appeal to my own memory impressions. Once again, then, I would accuse you of denying the legitimacy of the appeal to memory impressions as a mode of justification. In the terms of Wittgenstein's foregoing remarks, you deny my right to 'appeal from one memory to another.'

"You will undoubtedly say, with Wittgenstein, that you do not deny this right so long as the memory impression to which I appeal can 'itself be *tested* for correctness,' that in this case, it can indeed confirm another memory impression. But you will add that my memory impression of (private) sensations cannot thus be tested, since it can be tested only in ways that involve appeal to still other memory impressions of mine: 'justification consists in appealing to something independent.' You would, therefore, claim that the advocate of a PL_1 is like a man who checks upon the veracity of a newspaper report by reading another copy of the same report. I think, however, that the analogy is unfair. I admit that it is impossible for me to check any one of my memory impressions of sensations in any way that does not involve appeal to other memory impressions of mine. But how is any of us to find out anything at all about the past except by way of appeal to his own memory impressions? If you do not rely upon your memory impression that motion pictures have accurately recorded physical events in the past, what reason will you now have to treat a film that depicts a tree before you as evidence that there was a tree before you? How are you to confirm this memory impression unless you appeal to still other of your memory impressions? You deny the cognitive authority of my memory beliefs regarding my sensations just because I can check them only in ways that involve appeal to other of my memory beliefs. But how are you to check upon any of your memory beliefs regarding anything whatever unless you appeal to still other of your memory beliefs? I would suggest that there is no way in which you can do this. It seems to me that public language and PL_1 are in the same boat in this respect: Any check upon one's memory impressions must always involve appeal to other of one's memory impressions. Therefore, I conclude that you are committed to repudiate altogether the trustworthiness of memory and, thereby, to repudiate the possibility not only of PL_1 but of public language as well."

W: "How strange that you should think that a speaker of a public language cannot check upon his memory impressions in a way that involves no appeal to other memory impressions of his. If I seem to remember that there was a tree before me at 10 A.M., I can ask someone else whether this is true. If he says that he was present and remembers that the tree was before me at 10 A.M., then I have confirmed my memory impression, not by appeal to some other memory impression of mine, but by appeal to someone else's memory impression. By the same token, if I employ a film as a check upon my memory impression that there was a tree before me at 10 A.M., this need not involve appeal to my own memory impressions of past correlations between films and physical events (or other relevant correlations). I can ask others whether there have been such correlations, in which case it is not my memory impressions, but the memory impressions of other persons that give me reason to treat a film as evidence that confirms my memory impression regarding the tree. Alternatively, I can, in this way, check upon my own memory impressions of past correlations between films and physical events. Since I can check my memory impressions in ways that involve no appeal to other memory impressions of mine, that is, since I can have *independent* checks upon my memory impressions, it is proper that I trust my memory. Indeed, I have the right to 'appeal from one memory to another': for my memory impression of a railroad timetable or of a film can 'itself be *tested* for correctness' by appeal not to my own memory impressions but to the testimony of other persons as to what they remember.

"It is because you fail to notice the important differences between PL_1 and public language that you arrive at the erroneous conclusion that I am committed to repudiate the trustworthiness of memory and, thereby, the possibility of public language. The terms of a PL_1 are conceptually independent of publicly observable phenomena, that is, they are supposed to refer to private objects. It is for this reason that no one can know about the private experiential data of another, that no one else can understand the speaker of a PL_1, that a PL_1 is necessarily a PL_2. Since a PL_1 is necessarily a PL_2, the speaker of a PL_1 cannot utilize the testimony of other persons as a check upon his memory impressions of his experiential data. He therefore cannot check these memory impressions in any way that does not involve appeal to other memory impressions of his, that is, he cannot have *independent* checks upon these memory impressions. Hence, any checks that the PL_1-diarist employs are *uncheckable:* none of them can 'itself be *tested* for correctness.' So his would-be checks are not really checks at all. In contrast, none of this holds for one who speaks a *public* language. The descriptive terms of a public language (including the terms that refer to experiential data) are not conceptually independent of publicly observable phenomena: they refer not to private objects but to public objects. Although experiential data are not public in the same way that many physical situations are public, that is, they are not themselves publicly observable, they are publicly accessible—accessible to public knowledge—in that it is conceptually true that publicly observable phenomena provide evidence for their existence. Hence, a public-language speaker can utilize the testimony of other persons as a check upon his memory impressions either of physical situations or of his own (or others') experiential data. Thus, public language and PL_1 are not in the same boat: unlike the PL_1-diarist, one who speaks a public language can check upon his memory impressions of sensations in ways that do not involve appeal to other of his memory impressions. Since he can have *independent* checks upon his memory impressions, his checks upon his memory impressions are checkable: such a check, be it testimony, a film, or another memory impression of his, can 'itself be *tested* for correctness' and so is a genuine check. It is the diarist, not the public-language speaker, who has no right to trust his memory: it is PL_1, not public language, that is impossible."

T: "Since we are assuming, for purposes of our present stage of discussion, that a PL_1 is necessarily a PL_2, I am, of course, willing to grant you (for the present) that another person cannot know about my private experiential data, and, therefore, that I cannot utilize his testimony as a check on my memory impressions regarding my use of 'E' in my private diary. As you indicate, on the Wittgensteinian account of language, that is, public language, terms that refer to experiential data (or anything else) are not conceptually independent of publicly observable phenomena: so others can know about your sensations, and you can utilize their testimony as a check upon your memory impressions of your sensations (or of anything else). But I deny that such testimony will ever provide you with an independent check upon your memory impressions. I hold that the idea of independent checkability is a myth, that it is impossible, even for a speaker of a public language, to check upon any of one's memory impressions in a way that involves no appeal to other of one's memory impressions. This is why I think that you are, in fact, committed to repudiate the trustworthiness of memory and the possibility even of public language: since you demand as a condition of these that memory impressions be independently checkable, and since I hold such independent checks to be impossible, it seems to me that you have indeed incurred this commitment. Thus, although I admit that you can utilize the testimony of others as a check upon your memory impressions, and that I cannot do this with regard to my use of 'E' in my private diary, I am prepared to argue that public language and PL_1 are nevertheless in the same boat in the following respect: Neither you nor I can have independent checks upon our memory impressions, and, therefore, either you must admit that the impossibility of such checks does not render PL_1 impossible, or else you must confess yourself a total skeptic who denies the possibility not only of PL_1 but of public language as well.

"To begin this argument, I ask you what reason you have to believe the testimony of another person. Perhaps the person you consult in order to check upon your memory impressions is a liar or a fool. Surely his testimony will confirm your own memory impressions only if you have reason to believe that his word is reliable. How are you to establish the reliability of his testimony unless you appeal to your memory impressions concerning his past honesty and accuracy? Will you ask other people about him? This is only to shift your problem. You will have no better reason to believe them than you did the first person. Unless you have reason to believe that someone's testimony has been reliable in the past, you will have no reason to believe that it is reliable now, and so it will not serve as a check upon your own memory impressions. And what else but your own memory can justify you in believing that someone's testimony has hitherto been reliable? Nothing, I think. I would therefore insist that even when you employ the testimony of another person as a check upon your own memory impressions, you are using a check that involves appeal to your own memory impressions, and so you do not make use of an independent check."

4) The Testimony Thesis

W: "Following Wittgenstein's lead, Shoemaker and Malcolm have demonstrated the untenability of this line of argument.[12] Of course, I must have some reason to believe a person's testimony if it is to serve me as a check on my own memory impressions. But for this it is not necessary to establish empirically the reliability of his

---

[12] Cf. *Inv.*, 206–7, 226–27, 240–42; S. Shoemaker, *Self-Knowledge and Self-Identity* (Ithaca, N.Y.: Cornell University Press, 1963), pp. 229–39; Malcolm, "Memory and the Past," *Knowledge and Certainty, op. cit.*

word; for I know a priori that each person's memory claims are generally (i.e., preponderantly) true. This is a conceptual truth. More precisely stated, it is a conceptual truth that if a person makes memory claims, then the vast majority of his memory claims are true. Therefore, the mere fact that someone has testified that he remembers that there was a tree before me at 10 A.M. can give me some reason to believe that this is true, and so his testimony can serve as a check on my own memory impression of this matter. It may be that this person is a liar or that he has made an honest mistake; but there are ways of finding this out. Nor need I settle this question by appeal to my own memory; I can ask other people; I can give him a polygraph test. The reliability of the testimony of these other people has the same initial, a priori likelihood as the reliability of the first person. The reliability of the polygraph can be checked by appeal to the testimony of other persons and by means of other devices (e.g., films). Behind all of these various ways of checking the reliability of any one piece of testimony (or any one piece of evidence of any kind) lies the conceptual truth that memory claims are generally true. Since I know a priori that each person's memory claims are mostly true, the mere fact that one person makes such a claim can give me some initial reason to believe it, and by consulting a great many people, or employing other forms of evidence (e.g., films and fingerprints) whose reliability can itself be established by means of the testimony of many people, I can have very good reason to believe a particular piece of testimony. In this way, I can have independent checks on my memory impressions. If I could have reason to trust someone's word only if I had first established an empirical correlation between what he claims and what is the case, then, for just the reasons you have mentioned, testimony would not provide me with an independent check upon my own memory. Nor, in this case, would this be provided me by physical traces, such as films or fingerprints. But since I know a priori the conceptual truth that each person's memory claims are generally true, I can use the memory claims of others as a check upon my own without an empirical check upon their general reliability and hence without appeal to my own memory impressions. Thus, I may use not only testimony but also physical traces, such as ashes and fingerprints, as independent checks upon my own memory.

"Since any particular memory claim, such as 'There was a tree before you at 10 A.M.,' could well be false—that is, since, if it is true, it is an empirical (contingent) truth that is not known a priori—it would be a natural mistake to suppose that it is likewise not a conceptual (necessary) truth that we know a priori but an empirical (contingent) truth that we know a posteriori that each person's memory claims are generally true. That the latter is instead a conceptual (necessary) truth that we can know a priori may be seen in the following way. As we agreed (in Sec. 2), a person who is using language descriptively, for example, someone who is keeping a diary, must adhere to certain rules of the language. Thus, you agreed that the PL_1, in terms of which you propose to write your diary, is indeed a language only if you adhere to rules, such as the rule that you are to apply 'E' to those and only those experiential data that are of a certain kind. Similarly, a person is indeed testifying as to what he remembers—he is indeed making memory claims—only if his claims are usually true. Otherwise, there is not enough *regularity* of concomitance between what he says and what is the case—not enough adherence to rules of use (in this case, rules of claim-making or describing)—to qualify him as a language-speaker, as one who makes memory claims. If there is no regular correspondence between what he says and what has taken place in the past, then he is not making claims *about* the past. If almost all of the seeming memory claims of a child were false, he would properly be said never to have learned the language of making memory claims: he surely would not qualify for the category of one who speaks memory language but also is deceitful or has a poor memory. An explorer who proposed to translate the utterances of a newly discovered population in such a way that the vast majority of their supposed memory claims turned out false could only conclude that his proposed translation was incorrect. Nothing will serve to link a set of terms to the past, or to any other subject matter, in such a way that the terms refer to the subject matter unless there is a regular correspondence between the subject matter and the use of these terms. Therefore, we can know a priori the conceptual truth that a person's memory claims are mostly true, and so, in the way I have indicated, the testimony of others (and hence, too, physical traces) will provide me with independent checks upon my own memory impressions."

T: "It seems to me that your thesis (let us call it the *testimony thesis*) that it is an a priori, conceptual (necessary) truth that if a person makes memory claims then the vast majority of his memory claims are true, stands in need of considerable development, clarification, and qualification. Let me mention some of its difficulties.

(i) "It would seem that this thesis is incompatible with Shoemaker's claim that you appear to accept, 'That any particular sincere . . . memory statement is true is certainly a contingent matter . . .'[13] If I sincerely make

---

[13] Shoemaker, *op. cit.*, p. 229.

the particular memory claim 'I have been with other people in the past,' then if this claim were false, so many of my other putative memory claims would be false that, on the testimony thesis, I could not be said to make memory claims at all. So the testimony thesis appears to be incompatible with its being merely a contingent matter that this particular sincere memory statement is true.

(ii) "Another difficulty with the testimony thesis is this: Suppose that we have tampered with a person's brain during his infancy, or that he has a congenital neurological defect, so that throughout his life his memory claims are not usually true. Most of them, let us suppose, are close enough to the truth that there is no question but that he speaks the language (makes memory claims), but most of them involve some element of distortion, in which case each of these, taken as a whole, is false. For example, when he claims to remember having set a cup on his chair arm, he in fact set it on the table beside him; when he is right about where he set it, he is wrong about its size or its shape or its color. If such a situation is possible, as it seems to be, then the testimony thesis is not true as it stands.

(iii) "Still another and more serious problem for the testimony thesis is the following: Suppose that a person usually lies when he offers memory testimony to others, that is, when he makes memory claims, although his memory beliefs (or memory impressions) are mostly true. Shoemaker claims that '. . . it would be nonsense to suppose that people might always or generally lie.' [14] But since the person of our example is supposed to have mostly true memory beliefs, it is far from obvious that it is nonsense to suppose both that he makes memory

[14] *Ibid.*, p. 248.

claims and that his memory testimony is generally false. If his memory beliefs are generally true, then this would seem to provide enough regularity of concomitance between what he thinks, or says to himself, and what is the case, enough adherence to rules of descriptive use of the terms he employs in thinking, or talking to himself, to qualify him as a speaker of memory language and, hence, as one who makes memory claims, even though his memory claims are usually lies. If such a situation is possible, as it seems to be, then the testimony thesis is false."

W: "The third and last problem that you raise is the most important; but before turning to it let me consider in sequence the first two difficulties you mention.

"Regarding (i), the best way with your objection is to grant it, for it seems well taken and yet it will not damage my position. I am willing to admit that Shoemaker's claim is too broad as it stands and thus is incorrect: it is not the case that the truth of *any* particular memory statement (whether sincere or not) is a contingent matter. This is the case for a great many memory statements, such as the one I recently mentioned in this connection, 'There was a tree before you at 10 A.M.' But it does not hold for memory claims of much wider scope, such as the one you cite, or such as this one: '(I remember that) the earth is more than five minutes old.' As Malcolm and Wittgenstein have argued, the falsity of such a statement is inconceivable (conceptually impossible or senseless) since its falsity is 'incompatible with our concept of evidence,' since 'we cannot rationally think of it [i.e., the negation of the statement] as "possibly true." ' [15]

[15] Malcolm, "Memory and the Past," *op. cit.*, esp. pp. 199–202; also cf. *Inv.*, p. 221; N. Malcolm, *Ludwig Wittgenstein, a Memoir* (London: Oxford University Press, 1958), pp. 87–92.

Since such (apparent) memory claims cannot possibly be false, we could, if we wished, preserve Shoemaker's claim by denying that these very broad and general statements really count as memory claims and treat them as a peculiar brand of conceptual truth. But we also may, as I am perfectly willing to do, call them memory statements and admit that their truth is not a contingent matter. In either case, the existence of such statements is not incompatible with the testimony thesis.

"Regarding (ii), the situation that you depict is one wherein the person in question is 'close enough to the truth' in most of his memory claims 'that there is no question but that he speaks the language (makes memory claims).' If he is this close to the truth in most of his memory claims, then surely his testimony is reliable enough, in general, to serve as a check upon the memory impressions of others. Indeed, if most of his memory claims are this close to the truth, it is an artificial and arbitrary stratagem on your part to deny that most of his memory claims are true. Should you insist on speaking this way, I could get round the trivial difficulty you pose merely by qualifying the testimony principle to read: It is conceptually true that if a person makes memory claims then most of the component statements involved in his memory claims are true. Once this is seen, there seems to be nothing the matter with letting the testimony thesis stand as originally formulated. We can account for your fussy point by saying that the testimony thesis is nonetheless 'true as it stands,' for we shall treat it as embodying the qualification explicitly formulated in the above, alternative reading of the thesis. That yours is not a substantive criticism is clear from the fact that in order to insure 'that there is no question but that he (the person of your example) speaks the language (makes memory claims),' you were led to allow that the majority of his memory claims are 'close enough to the truth.'

"Let me now address myself to (iii). If I speak a public language, the descriptive terms of my language refer to public objects or public states of affairs (be they mental or physical) that are accessible to public knowledge. Thus, I can utilize the testimony of others as a check on my own memory impressions. None of this have you denied. You wish to show that it is nevertheless impossible that I have independent checks upon my memory impressions. To this end, you dispute my testimony thesis by arguing that it is possible that others usually lie when making memory claims. But if it is possible that others usually lie, then I could never distinguish a person's generally offering deceitful memory claims from his emitting utterances that sound like memory claims but, in fact, are not memory claims; that is, I could not possibly have reason to accept one of these alternatives rather than the other. So if it were possible that a person usually lies in giving memory testimony, then it would not be possible for me to know whether another person is a chronic liar or whether he has failed to master the language and is merely emitting utterances. Therefore, unless you are prepared to retract what you seem already to have accepted—the obvious truth that a speaker of a public language can know about public matters, such as the beliefs of others, that he can know whether or not another is lying, and whether or not another is making claims—you must admit that it is impossible that a person usually lies when he makes memory claims. But if you admit this, your argument in (iii) fails: in accordance with the testimony thesis, we Wittgensteinians maintain that lying must be the exception

—cannot be the rule—and that the case you offer as a possibility must be characterized by saying that the hypothetical person of your example has never mastered the memory language and so does not make memory claims."

T: "Your reply to my criticisms of the testimony thesis seems rather effective, and I am prepared to grant you the testimony thesis as the statement of a conceptual truth of public language. But even though I do so, I would still maintain that you cannot have independent checks upon your memory impressions. It might now appear that this is possible: it would seem that since you can know a priori that the memory claims of others are generally true, the testimony of others will provide you with independent checks upon your memory impressions and so also, therefore, will physical traces. It is important to notice, however, that the testimony thesis does not state that there is, in fact, some testimony, or this or that particular piece of testimony. It is a *conditional* proposition that says: *If* a person makes memory claims, then the vast majority of his memory claims are true. Hence, the testimony thesis by itself will not provide you with an independent check upon any memory impression of yours, for example, your impression that there was a tree before you at 10 A.M. In order to have such a check, you must have reason to believe that another person has made a memory claim, for example, the claim, 'There was a tree before you at 10 A.M.' What reason can you have to think that someone has made such a claim? Let us suppose that a body rather like yours—let us call such bodies *human bodies*—has emitted the *sounds* (the *utterance*), 'There was a tree before you at 10 A.M.' Surely you can have reason to believe that this human body is the body of a person who is making a memory claim—who speaks a language and is offering testimony—only if you establish this empirically. What empirical reason can you have to believe this? Surely you can have empirical evidence on this matter only if you have reason to believe that in the past there has been a regular correspondence between the utterances of such bodies and the happenings prior to such utterances. How else can you have reason to believe that this is a person who knows the language and is making a memory claim, rather than merely a body producing certain noises? Surely the fact, if it is a fact, that there is a person who is making a memory claim, is an empirical fact and is not to be known a priori. But if you can know or have reason to believe that someone has made a memory claim only if you have empirical reason to believe that certain correlations have held in the past, then it is only in ways that involve appeal to other of your memory impressions that you can have reason to believe that someone's testimony confirms (or disconfirms) your own memory impression. How, otherwise, are you to establish such past correlations? Will you appeal to the testimony of some other person? This merely duplicates your initial problem: the same difficulties that hold for the first person will hold for the second person.

"So, I grant you the testimony thesis. You can know a priori that if someone gives you memory testimony, then what he says is probably true. Therefore, if you can know that someone has made a memory claim, and if you can know this in a way that involves no appeal to your own memory, then you can have independent checks upon your own memory impressions. But I deny that you can know this in this way, and so I deny that you can have independent checks upon your memory, even given the truth of the testimony thesis."

5) The Utterance Thesis[16]

W: "You are quite right when you maintain that my a priori knowledge of the (conditional) testimony thesis will not by itself enable me to have independent checks upon my memory impressions. As you say, I must also have reason to believe that someone has offered memory testimony—has made a memory claim—and I cannot know this a priori: that someone has made a memory claim is an empirical matter, and so if I am to have reason to believe that someone has made a memory claim, then I must have empirical reason to believe this. But I deny that I can have empirical reason to believe that someone has made a memory claim only if I have empirical reason to believe that certain correlations have obtained in the past. If you were right about this, then, for just the reasons you mention, it would indeed be impossible that I have independent checks upon my memory impressions. How else can I have empirical reason to believe that someone has made a memory claim? His utterance gives me this reason. More precisely, the fact that a body like mine, a *human body* as you say, emits an utterance, like the utterances that I myself employ in making statements, is an empirical fact in virtue of which I can have some reason to believe that someone has made a statement. If his utterance is like the utterances that I use in making memory claims, then it can give me some reason to believe that he has made

[16] This thesis has been developed in Shoemaker, *op. cit.*, pp. 247–54. Cf. Wittgenstein, *Inv.*, 206–7, 244–45, 386, 465–87, 503–7, 594, pp. 178–80, 226–27.

a memory claim. My reason will, of course, be empirical rather than a priori: it is the empirical fact of his utterance being similar to certain of mine that entitles me to believe that he makes a memory claim.

"Notice that I say it *entitles* me: it is not 'reason to believe' in the sense that I draw an inference from this fact (although this too would entitle me to believe); it is 'reason to believe' in the sense that it is in virtue of this fact that I am reason*able* in believing (have the right to believe) that he makes a memory claim (cf. *Inv.*, 289). Notice, too, that it might be less misleading were we to say with Shoemaker and Wittgenstein that it is not that I *believe* that this is a person who is speaking a language (rather than merely a body that is emitting sounds), but rather that this is my *attitude*.

> It is, I should like to say, part of our 'form of life,' to use Wittgenstein's expression, that we accept what other persons say at face value, without normally raising or even considering the question whether they understand the meanings of the expressions they utter, or whether their apparent testimony is really testimony. Normally there is no inference, and certainly not an inductive inference, from 'He uttered the sounds "I went for a walk yesterday"' to 'He said that he went for a walk yesterday.' We regard a person who is talking, not as making sounds from which, knowing the circumstances in which such sounds have been uttered in the past, we can make certain inductive inferences, but as *saying something*. We regard what he says as *having meaning*, not simply in the sense in which a barometer reading has meaning, i.e., as indicating that something has happened, is happening, or is about to happen, but as expressing what *he* means. It would be misleading to describe this as a *belief* on our part, the belief that people who use the words we use generally mean by them what we mean by them. It is rather a matter of attitude, of the way in which we respond to a person who is talking. (Here

I am guided by Wittgenstein's remark: 'My attitude towards him is an attitude towards a soul. I am not of the opinion that he has a soul.' [*Inv.*, p. 178]) If this attitude were one of belief, we could inquire into the grounds of the belief. But this is just what we do not do. It is part of the expression of this attitude that the question of what justifies us in regarding what others say as testimony does not arise. We say 'I heard him say that he will come,' not 'I heard him utter the sounds "I will come," and gathered from this that he was saying that he would come.' [17]

Having called attention to ways in which using 'belief,' rather than 'attitude,' can mislead, I shall in future feel free to use either of these terms in discussing the reasonableness of regarding an utterance as testimony.

"Let me formulate in the following way the main principle with which I am presently concerned. Let us call this the *utterance thesis:* It is an a priori, conceptual (necessary) truth that if one has reason to believe that a human body has produced an utterance like those one uses to make statements (e.g., memory claims), then one has some initial reason to believe that there is another person whose body this is and who has used this utterance to make a statement like those one makes with similar utterances (e.g., memory utterances). Briefly and roughly stated, the utterance thesis says that it is a conceptual truth that human utterances (e.g., memory utterances) provide evidence for the existence of statements (e.g., memory claims). An utterance 'provides evidence' not in the sense that one draws an inference from the fact that there is such an utterance but in the sense that it is in virtue of the utterance that one is entitled to believe (i.e., has reason to believe, or is reasonable in one's attitude) that another person has made a statement

[17] Shoemaker, *op. cit.*, pp. 249–50.

(or claim). An utterance 'provides evidence' in that it is a priori true that such an utterance confers an initial likelihood upon the proposition that another person is making a claim. This proposition may be false in a particular instance. It may be that a certain body that emits the utterance, 'There was a tree before you at 10 A.M.,' is not the body of a person who is making a memory claim but is the body of a human who has not mastered a language and who is not making a statement. But there are ways of finding this out: the initial likelihood of the proposition in question may be increased or decreased by additional data.

"In light of the testimony thesis, I know a priori that the mere fact that another person makes a memory claim that p confers some initial probability upon p. In light of the utterance thesis, I know a priori that the mere fact that another human body emits an utterance 'p,' like those I use to make the memory claim that p, confers some initial probability upon the proposition that another person is making a memory claim that p. Hence, I know a priori that the mere fact that another human body emits an utterance 'p,' like those I use to make the memory claim that p, confers some initial probability upon the proposition that p. Hence, the utterances of other human bodies can give me reason to believe that other persons have made memory claims that p, and, thereby, reason to believe that p. My reason will be empirical reason, for it is an empirical matter that there are utterances and that there are memory claims. Thus, I can have independent checks upon my memory impressions. In virtue of the utterances of other bodies, I can have reason to think that other persons are making memory claims. In virtue of the memory claims of other persons, I can have reason to think that various propositions about the past are true. It is in this way that the testimony of others can provide me with independent checks upon my own memory impressions. Hence, too, physical traces (e.g., ashes and egg stains) will provide independent checks upon my memory: for their evidential value can be established by appeal not necessarily to my own memory beliefs but to the memory beliefs of others. Particular utterances, claims, and traces may mislead, but this can be discovered by means of more of the same: by consulting a great many people, I can have very good reason to rely upon a particular physical trace or a particular piece of testimony."

T: "Let me recapitulate the recent course of our discussion.

"You maintain that since a PL_1 is a PL_2, I, as a speaker of a PL_1, cannot use the testimony of others to check upon my memory impressions. Lacking such testimony, I cannot have independent checks upon my memory impressions and therefore my PL_1 (e.g., my private diary) is impossible. Because I cannot have independent checks on my memory impressions, my alleged checks are not checkable and so are not genuine checks. Thus, my alleged memory impressions are not really memory impressions, and I cannot properly be said to trust my memory. My alleged language is not a language.

"I contend that PL_1 and public language are in the same boat in that it is impossible for a speaker of either kind of language to have independent checks upon his memory impressions. Thus, I maintain that if you are to repudiate the idea of a PL_1 because its speaker can have no independent checks on his memory impressions, then, for the same reason, you must also repudiate the idea of a public language. I do not see that the impossibility of independent checks upon one's memory impressions destroys the possibility of one's speaking a language. Since you do take this position, then if I am right in thinking that even a speaker of a public language cannot have independent checks upon his memory impressions, you shall have committed yourself to the absurdly skeptical idea that both PL_1 and public language are impossible.

"You have tried to meet this criticism by showing that it is possible that you, as a speaker of public language, have independent checks upon your memory impressions. Your latest move in this direction is to advance the utterance thesis. You hold that it is a priori true that certain utterances count as evidence (give some reason to believe) that other persons are making memory claims. Since, according to the testimony thesis, if someone gives you memory testimony then what he says is probably true, you think that the utterance thesis will enable you to have independent checks upon your memory impressions: the utterances of others can give you reason to believe that they are making memory claims that are probably true, and so their testimony will serve as an independent check upon your memory impressions.

"I wish now to argue, however, that even though you accept the utterance thesis as the statement of a conceptual truth of public language, this will not enable you, as a speaker of public language, to have independent checks upon your memory impressions. I do not think that the utterance thesis will allow you to check upon your memory impressions in a way that involves no appeal to other of your memory impressions. I grant you that if you have reason to believe that another human body has emitted a memory utterance, that is, an utterance like those that you use to make memory claims (e.g., the utterance, 'There was a tree before you at 10 A.M.'), then you will have some initial reason to believe that another person has made a memory claim that is probably true, and so you will have some reason to think that your own memory impressions on this matter are (to some extent) confirmed or disconfirmed. Thus, I grant you that if you have reason to believe in the existence of a certain utterance (e.g., the utterance, 'There was a tree before you at 10 A.M.'), then you will have a check upon your own memory. But I deny that this is an independent check: what reason can you have to believe in the existence of this utterance? Will you appeal to your memory impression of the occurrence of this utterance? But then your check upon your original memory impression is not an independent check: it involves appeal to other of your memory impressions. Perhaps you will object that you need not appeal to your memory impression of what was said, that you may now be hearing the utterance, in which case such appeal is unnecessary. But are you hearing the first portion of the utterance at the time at which you are hearing the last portion of the utterance? Presumably not. So you will still have to appeal to your own memory in support of the idea that there exists such an utterance. You may object that you can hear the entire utterance and that it is absurd to suppose that it is your memory impression of (at least) portions of the utterance that gives you reason to believe in the occurrence of part or all of the utterance. But even if this were so, checking upon one's memory impression is not a process that necessarily lasts no longer than the second or two during which one hears a relatively brief utterance. Surely the utterance will not serve as a check at all unless you can still have reason, several seconds later, to believe in the occurrence of the utterance. And what reason can you then have to believe this unless you are willing to appeal to your memory impression(s) of the utterance? You may say of those memory impressions of yours upon which you must rely (i.e., to which you must appeal either explicitly or implicitly) if you are to have reason to believe in the existence of this human utterance, that they themselves can be checked by appeal to still other human utterances. But this will not help: what has held true of this utterance will (for the same reasons) hold true of any other utterances, and therefore no appeal to human utterances will provide you with an independent check upon your memory impressions."

6) The Nature of Independent Checks

W: "In order to meet this last objection of yours, we shall have to get very clear on just what it is to have an independent check upon a memory impression. We have both described an independent check as a check that involves no appeal to other of one's memory impressions. The time has come to unpack this idea. If something serves one as a check upon one's memory impression that p, it provides one with evidence that p (or that not-p). By an *independent* check I mean a check whose evidential value (i.e., evidence-affording status) can be established without appeal to one's own memory impressions. That one have any such checks requires that one can have checks whose evidential value is an a priori, conceptual matter rather than an empirical matter. As a public-language speaker, the memory claims and memory utterances of others provide me with checks of the latter sort. The utterance thesis confers this evidential status on the memory utterances of other human bodies, and the testimony thesis confers this evidential status on the memory claims of other persons. The fact that these two theses state conceptual truths of the public language I speak enables me to employ the memory utterances of other human bodies and, thereby, the memory claims of other persons as checks whose evidential value is an a priori, conceptual matter rather than an empirical matter. Thus, the testimony of other persons provides me with an independent check upon my own memory impressions, that is, a check whose evidential value can be established without appeal to my own memory impressions. So too, therefore, do physical traces, such as films and footprints, provide me with an independent check upon my own memory impressions. For the evidential value of physical traces can be established without appeal to one's own memory impressions, even though their evidential value, unlike that of testimony, is an empirical matter and not an a priori, conceptual matter: their evidential value can be established by appeal to the testimony of others to the effect that such traces have in the past been correlated with situations of certain kinds. Since the testimony of others can give me reason to believe in the existence of empirical correlations that confer evidential value upon physical traces, I can establish their evidential value without appeal to my own memory impressions. Thus, both physical traces and testimony serve me as independent checks upon my memory, although the evidential value of the former is an empirical matter, whereas the evidential value of the latter is an a priori matter.

"Testimony is the most fundamental kind of independent check, for I know a priori that the memory claims (and memory utterances) of other persons have evidential value. Physical traces constitute a derivative kind of independent check since I can only know empirically the evidential value of physical traces of any specified kind and since it is only by appeal to the testimony of others that I can establish this without appeal to my own memory impressions. Thus, it is that testimony plays a fundamental role in public language: The a priori evidential value of the memory claims (and memory utterances) of other persons makes their testimony an independent check upon my memory impressions, and it enables me to establish empirically the evidential value of physical traces (without appeal to my own memory impressions) so that these, too, will serve me as independent checks upon my memory. (As Shoemaker indicates,[18] the perceptual claims and utterances of others likewise provide a public-language speaker with testimony whose evidential value is an a priori matter that he can use as an independent check upon his own beliefs. Here, however, I propose to concentrate upon the role of memory testimony in public language.)

"Now to turn to your objection. You wish to say that since I must rely upon my own memory when using someone's testimony to check upon a memory impression of mine, even the testimony of others will not provide me with an independent check upon my memory impression. In particular, you contend that since I can use the testimony of another only if my memory impressions entitle me to regard him as having made a certain utterance, my check upon my memory impression is not an independent check: it involves appeal to other of my memory impressions. In reply, I have spelled out my conception of an independent check as a check whose evidential value can be established without appeal to one's own memory impressions. Since the evidential value of another's utterance can be established without appeal to my own memory impressions—since the utterance thesis (in conjunction with the testimony thesis)

---

[18] Shoemaker, *op. cit.,* pp. 229–39, 247–54.

confers upon it an a priori evidential value—another's utterance will, indeed, serve me as an independent check upon my memory impression.

"You will object, I am sure, that my conception of an independent check will not at all do. We have both described an independent check as a check which involves *no* appeal to one's own memory impressions. You have pointed out that even though memory utterances have an a priori evidential value for a speaker of public language, he will nevertheless have to rely upon his memory in using an utterance (and thereby testimony) as a check upon his memory impression. So you will say that when I, as a public-language speaker, utilize testimony as a check upon my memory impression, my check involves appeal to other of my memory impressions and therefore is not an independent check. Thus, you would, no doubt, repudiate my present conception of an independent check as a departure from what we have hitherto meant by 'independent check,' and as question-begging in that it redefines this term in such a way as to settle in my favor the issue between us.

"I am perfectly willing to admit that you are correct when you maintain that the very idea of checking upon one's memory impression, even for one who speaks a public language, is an idea that involves one's appeal to or reliance upon other of one's memory impressions. This is so for just the reasons you have mentioned: even when I use someone else's testimony as a check upon my memory impression, I am entitled so to use his testimony only if other of my memory impressions entitle me to regard him as having made a certain memory utterance. Although, as you say, I could object that sometimes we rely upon testimony we are hearing at the time so that we need not then rely upon our memories but only upon our senses in order to be justified in believing in the occurrence of the testimony, there is little point to my making this objection. For, as you indicate, checking can take time, and if I am to use testimony to check upon my memory impression, it must be that my memory impressions either do or will entitle me to believe in the occurrence of the testimony. (This is not, of course, to subscribe to the position that inner acts of remembering, or recognizing, are occurring when I understand someone's words—or recognize a physical trace (cf. *Inv.*, 166, 601–4). It is only to grant the indispensable cognitive role one's own memory plays when, for example, one is entitled to believe that one has just heard some testimony.) So, to put the 'do or will' matter briefly, I shall grant you that I must rely upon my memory in checking upon my memory: I shall grant you that I am entitled to use someone's memory claim as a check upon my memory impression only if other of my memory impressions entitle me to regard him as having made a certain memory utterance. (Of course, it may be that it is a physical trace, or yet another person's testimony, that entitles me to believe that the first person made a certain memory claim; but if none of my memory impressions justifies me in believing that a physical trace or a human utterance—or inscription, etc.—has occurred, then I shall have no reason to believe that the first person has made a memory claim.)

"Unless one is to adopt the absurdly skeptical position that one has no right to trust one's memory, unless one is to embrace the absurd idea of a language in which one's memory impressions carry no cognitive authority, one must accept the following idea: It is a conceptual truth that in checking upon one's memory impression(s) one must rely upon or appeal (at least implicitly) to other of one's memory impressions. But since this is a priori true for a speaker of *any* language, be it a PL_1

or a public language, it seems to me an unremarkable similarity between PL_1 and public language that in both languages the idea of checking upon one's memory impression(s) is an idea that involves one's appeal to or reliance upon other of one's memory impressions. It was not this that I wished to deny when I said that, unlike one who speaks a PL_1, a public-language speaker can utilize the testimony of others as a check upon his memory impressions and so can have independent checks upon them. Rather, I wished to deny that a public-language speaker is like a PL_1-speaker in that it is only by way of appeal to his own memory impressions that he can establish the evidential value of his checks upon his memory impressions. Thus, when I said that a public-language speaker can avail himself of the testimony of others and thereby check upon his memory impressions in a way that involves no appeal to other of his memory impressions, I meant that he need not appeal to his own memory impressions in order to establish the evidential value of others' testimony (of their memory claims and utterances). This is not to say that he need not 'appeal to' (at least implicitly rely upon) his own memory impressions in order to have reason to believe that someone has given testimony (has made a memory claim or utterance). That he must do this, I grant you. But I think that this is essential to the idea of speaking a language, for it is essential to the idea of trusting our memories: neither you nor I have wished to deny the fundamental, cognitive status of memory.

"Thus, I grant you that PL_1 and public language are in the same boat in this respect: reliance upon one's memory is essential to the idea of checking upon one's memory impressions. If you construe 'independent check' so broadly that it is incompatible with one's checking by means of remembered testimony, then, on this definition of 'independent check,' not even a speaker of public language can have independent checks upon his memory impressions. It is precisely this that makes this way of defining 'independent check' uninteresting: it brings out an unremarkable similarity between PL_1 and public language. PL_1 and public language are not, however, in the same boat in the following respect: a public-language speaker can, whereas a PL_1-speaker cannot, establish the evidential value of a check upon his memory impressions without appeal to other of his memory impressions. If we construe 'independent check' more narrowly, as I suggest, then a public-language speaker can, whereas a PL_1-speaker cannot, have independent checks upon his memory impressions. It is precisely this that makes this way of defining 'independent check' interesting: it brings out a crucial difference between PL_1 and public language.

"I grant you that it was misleading of me to insist that a public-language speaker can check upon his memory impressions in ways that 'involve no appeal to other of his memory impressions.' I grant you that it was misleading of me to use this quoted phrase as a way of characterizing the notion of an independent check. Indeed, I must confess that I was then only groping toward the more satisfactory conception of an independent check that I have just presented. But now that I have attempted to clarify my ideas on this matter, and now that I have granted you that even a public-language speaker cannot have independent checks in the broader and less interesting sense of 'independent check,' surely you must admit that a public-language speaker *can* have independent checks in the narrower and more interesting sense of this phrase—the sense of this phrase that I now offer as my conception of an independent check. He can employ checks whose evidential value does not rest upon, that is, is independent of, his own memory. It is for this reason that, unlike the PL$_1$-speaker, he can have genuine checks upon his memory impressions: as Wittgenstein says, 'justification consists in appealing to something independent' (*Inv.*, 265). This 'something independent,' be it testimony or a physical trace, is independent in that its evidential value can be established without appeal to one's own memory impressions.[19] It has this inde-

---

[19] The Wittgensteinian has emphasized the idea that testimony is the most fundamental kind of independent check, and that physical traces constitute a derivative kind of independent check. He has said that this is so because memory claims (and memory utterances) have an a priori evidential value, whereas the evidential value of any specified kind of physical trace is an empirical matter. It could be objected that, strictly speaking, physical traces are not independent checks: for in order to establish the evidential value of a physical trace, A, by means of someone's memory claim that A and B have been correlated in the past, one must rely upon (at least implicitly appeal to) one's own memory impression(s) of the occurrence of this memory claim. In reply, the Wittgensteinian may allow the correctness of the objection: it will nevertheless remain true that a public-language speaker can utilize the testimony of others as an independent check upon his memory impressions. Alternatively, the Wittgensteinian might choose to redefine "independent check" as: either testimony or a check whose evidential value can be established by appeal to testimony. The latter alternative seems preferable to the former, since it permits, not only testimony, but also physical traces to be placed in the category of independent checks. So long as it is realized that the Wittgensteinian can easily make this slight modification in his definition of "independent check," it will be most convenient to allow the dialogue to continue without changing the latest formulation of the meaning of "independent check," viz., a check whose evidential value can be established without appeal to one's own memory impressions. It should also be noted that throughout the discussion it is tacitly (and properly) assumed that an independent check upon one's memory impression can never be another of one's memory impressions—even though it is a priori true that one is, in general, entitled to trust one's memory.

pendence, that is, this check that one uses is an independent check, even though in using this check one is involved in an appeal to or reliance upon one's memory in the following way: it is one's memory impressions of the occurrence of this check, or of the occurrence of the testimony or physical traces, that justify one in believing in the occurrence of this check, that entitle one to believe in the occurrence of this check. The fact that a PL_1-speaker cannot have such independent checks at once distinguishes PL_1 from public language and renders impossible a PL_1."

7) Unchecked Checks and Uncheckable Checks

T: "I understand how you want to use the expression 'independent check': you want to say that even though one relies upon, or is involved in an appeal to, one's own memory in using a check, the check one uses will nevertheless be an independent check if its evidential value can be established without appeal to one's own memory. I am perfectly willing to accept this way of talking and to employ this conception of an independent check. Hence, I shall now agree with you that PL_1 and public language are not in the same boat in that a speaker of public language can, and a PL_1-speaker cannot, have independent checks upon his memory impressions. But while I grant you that this distinguishes public language from PL_1, I deny that this means that public language is possible whereas PL_1 is impossible. For while I grant you this difference, in light of the meaning you have given to 'independent check,' it nevertheless remains true, as you have allowed, that PL_1 and public language are in the same boat in that neither a public-language speaker nor a PL₁-speaker can use something as a check upon his memory without reliance upon, or appeal to, his own memory. Far from its being an uninteresting or unremarkable similarity between PL₁ and public language, as you assert, this seems to me to be a crucial similarity between them. I think it is because of this similarity that you must either abandon your attack upon PL₁, and admit its possibility, or else you must confess yourself a total skeptic who denies the possibility of public language as well. I wish to contend that the fact that you, as a public-language speaker, can have independent checks upon your memory impressions, whereas I, as a PL₁-speaker, cannot, does not have an important bearing upon the issue at hand.

"Suppose that someone tells you that there was, indeed, a tree before you at 10 A.M., and that you use this as a check upon your memory impression regarding the tree. To keep things simple, suppose that you check no further: you neither seek the testimony of anyone else, for example, nor do you check upon your memory impression of this person's testimony. Compare a case in which I use a physiological chart as a check upon my memory impression of a (private) sensation. To keep things simple, suppose that I check no further: I neither consult any other charts, for example, nor do I check upon my memory impression of this chart. Admittedly, you employ an independent check and I do not: the evidential value of your check can be established without appeal to your own memory impressions whereas that of mine cannot. Why does this seem to me an unimportant difference? Because, despite this difference, neither your check nor mine is worth any more than the memory impressions of ours that entitle us to believe in the existence of these checks. If your memory impression of the testimony is mistaken, then your check will not serve its purpose, and similarly for my memory impression of the chart. What does it matter that the evidential value of my chart depends upon my memory whereas the evidential value of the testimony you use does not depend upon your memory, when your epistemic right to believe that someone has given a particular piece of testimony depends upon your memory, just as my epistemic right to believe that there was a certain chart-reading depends upon my memory? As Wittgenstein says: 'Justification by experience comes to an end. If it did not it would not be justification.' [20] At its end will lie unchecked checks, that is, checks whose existence is attested by nothing other than one's own memory impressions of these checks. Either these memory impressions entitle us to accept the existence of these checks or they do not. If they do, they do for both you and me, and if they do not then they do not for both you and me: for these are memory impressions that neither of us check upon. Therefore, either the checking process in a PL_1 is legitimate and a PL_1 is possible, or else the checking process in a public language is likewise illegitimate and a public language is likewise impossible. If unchecked memory impressions will serve in the one they will serve in the other. And if it is legitimate to rely upon unchecked memory impressions, then surely it is legitimate to rely upon nonindependent checks, that is, checks whose evidential value cannot be established without appeal to one's own memory impressions. Conversely, if it is illegitimate to rely upon nonindependent checks, then surely it is illegitimate to rely upon unchecked checks, that is, checks whose existence is attested by nothing other than one's memory impressions of the checks.

---

[20] *Inv.*, 485. Cf. *Inv.*, 1, 84–7; 211–13, 217, 228, 292.

You can deny the possibility of a PL_1 on grounds of the illegitimacy of its nonindependent checks only at the price of commitment to the impossibility of public language in virtue of the illegitimacy of its unchecked checks."

W: "I think I see what you are getting at. With regard to the hypothetical cases you offer for our consideration, you admit that my check (the testimony), unlike your check (the chart), has an evidential value that does not depend upon appeal to one's own memory. But you point out that if I am wrong about the nature of my check, then it will nevertheless fail to serve its purpose, and that it is only my own memory impression that entitles me to believe that the check is of a certain sort (that there was, indeed, a certain piece of testimony), since the check is an unchecked check. Thus, my checking process can be no more effective than my unchecked memory impression of the testimony that I use as a check. Since checks always must come to an end, this must always be the case. You wish to say that since a checking process is of no more epistemic worth than the memory impressions that entitle us to accept the unchecked checks at the end of the process, we are therefore no more entitled to use independent checks than we are to use nonindependent checks. In each case, you contend, the epistemic worth of all of our checking must rest upon our own memories, so that either nonindependent checks are legitimate or no checks are legitimate: either a PL_1 is possible or no language is possible.

"I think, however, that you have fallen into the sort of error of which Anscombe has accused Ayer.[21] It is

[21] Cf. G. E. M. Anscombe, *An Introduction to Wittgenstein's Tractatus* (London: Hutchinson and Co. Ltd., 1959), pp. 138–39; A. J. Ayer, *op. cit.*, pp. 41–3; A. J. Ayer, *The Problem of*

perfectly true that it is impossible, and hence unnecessary, to check every one of one's checks: checking has an end, and at its end lie unchecked checks. But it would be a mistake to think that one can logically move from this truth to the (false) proposition that it is impossible, and hence unnecessary, to have checks every one of which is checkable. Of course, not every check is checked; but it does not follow that it is legitimate to employ uncheckable checks. You and I, alike, employ unchecked checks. In what way must both of our checking processes contain unchecked checks? We will both, as you say, employ some checks whose existence is attested by nothing other than our own memory impressions of these checks: in your examples, this is the case for your chart and for the testimony I use. But your checks, unlike mine, are uncheckable. In what way are your checks uncheckable whereas mine are not? Your checks, unlike mine, are uncheckable in that their evidential value cannot be established without appeal to one's own memory impressions: in your examples, this is the case for your chart (whose evidential value rests upon remembered correlations) but not for the testimony I use (whose evidential value is an a priori matter). Your checks, unlike mine, are uncheckable and hence are not genuine checks because you cannot, whereas I can, have independent checks.

"So I grant you that our languages have the unremarkable similarity that we both employ some unchecked checks. These checks are unchecked in the sense that their existence is attested by nothing other than our own memory impressions of these checks. It is a conceptual truth that such unchecked checks will lie at the end of

Knowledge (Harmondsworth: Penguin Books, 1956), pp. 60–61; A. P. Griffiths, "Ayer on Perception," *Mind*, LXIX (Oct., 1960), 497–98.

a checking process, and there is nothing disturbing in this fact. But our languages also have the remarkable dissimilarity that your checks are uncheckable and mine are not. Yours are uncheckable in the sense that their evidential value cannot be established without appeal to your own memory impressions whereas mine are not thus uncheckable. Since, as Wittgenstein says, 'justification consists in appealing to something independent' (*Inv.*, 265), and since you cannot appeal to independent checks, to checks that are in this sense checkable, your alleged checks are not genuine checks: they are not checks at all. Thus, the fact that I can have independent checks whereas you cannot is responsible for the fact that my public language is possible whereas your PL_1 is not."

T: "It is, of course, one thing to say that a check is unchecked and another to say that it is uncheckable, and the latter does not follow from the former. Thus, were I to have confused these two things, in particular, were I to have thought that the possibility or legitimacy of uncheckable checks follows—simply by the rules of modal logic—from the possibility or legitimacy of unchecked checks, I should indeed have fallen into the error of which Anscombe accuses Ayer. But my argument is more subtle than this. I contend that since we must rely upon our unchecked memory impressions in using those unchecked checks that lie at the end of any checking process, it would be arbitrary to deny the legitimacy of reliance upon our memory impressions in establishing the evidential value of the items we use to check upon our memory impressions. Yes, your checks are checkable and mine are not in the sense you have given to 'checkable check': namely, you can establish the evidential value of your checks without appeal to your own memory impressions. In other words, you can and I cannot have independent checks in the sense you have given to 'independent check.' But this much you and I have agreed upon for some time. Where we disagree is over the question of whether a PL_1 is impossible in virtue of the fact that a PL_1-speaker cannot have independent (or checkable) checks upon his memory impressions. So it will not do for you to accuse me of having committed a rather simple-minded modal fallacy that involves confusing 'checked' and 'checkable.' You must show that a PL_1 is impossible by showing that nonindependent checks are not really checks. This you have claimed but have not shown. It simply doesn't follow from the fact that the presuppositions of my language (a PL_1) are not identical with those of your language (a public language) that my language is impossible and hence not a language. It means only that a PL_1 is not a *public* language, and this, you must allow, is an extremely unexciting thing for you to have proved.

"In particular, you have not really met my criticism that even if a public-language speaker has independent checks upon his memory impressions, his checks will be of no more epistemic worth to him than his unchecked memory impressions that entitle him to accept the existence of his unchecked checks. My point is that if this reliance upon his own memory is legitimate, then so is the reliance upon memory of a PL_1-speaker who can have no independent checks. To provide a satisfactory answer to this criticism, you must surely do more than point to the rules of modal logic: presumably, you will have to adduce sophisticated epistemological considerations."

8) *Are Nonindependent Checks Legitimate?*

W: "The fundamental epistemological reason why non-independent checks are not really checks is that they leave no room for a distinction between objective and subjective reality, between how things are and how they seem to one to be. This is so because an alleged check upon one's memory impression, if its evidential value derives and can derive only from other of one's memory impressions, is not really a check upon one's memory impression. It is, as Wittgenstein indicates, like buying another copy of the morning paper (*Inv.*, 265). How can it be a check upon one's memory when it is not an appeal to 'something independent'? Thus, Wittgenstein admonishes us: 'Always get rid of the idea of the private object in this way: assume that it constantly changes, but that you do not notice the change because your memory constantly deceives you' (*Inv.*, p. 207). There can be no distinction between objective and subjective reality for a PL_1-speaker just because he can have no way of telling whether his memory is constantly deceiving him: his only way of telling would be his memory, and so this would not be a way of telling. 'One would like to say: whatever is going to seem right to me is right. And that only means that here we can't talk about "right" ' (*Inv.*, 258).

"Throughout our discussion I have again and again adduced these considerations. I therefore wonder at your charge that I have merely claimed but have not shown that nonindependent checks are not really checks. I shall take your word that you have not been enticed by what

you have called 'a rather simple-minded modal fallacy.'
But how are you to overcome these *epistemological* considerations? Presumably you hope to do so by means of
the criticism of my position to which you have just referred: you say that if the reliance upon one's memory
that is involved in the (inevitable) use of unchecked
checks is legitimate for a speaker of public language,
then so is the reliance upon memory of a PL₁-speaker
who can have no independent checks. Let me now address myself to this criticism.

"We have agreed that the former sort of reliance upon
one's memory is unavoidable: that it is a conceptual
truth that the idea of a checking process involves the
idea of one's reliance upon unchecked memory impressions. Being unavoidable, being part of the very idea of
checking upon one's memory impressions, it in no way
goes to show that one's checking process is illegitimate.
It is for this reason that it is an unremarkable similarity
between PL₁ and public language that speakers of both
sorts of language must rely in this way upon their own
memories when checking upon their memory impressions.
In contrast, however, there is another sort of reliance
upon one's own memory that is avoidable for a public-
language speaker but not for one who speaks a PL₁: it
is a conceptual truth that the former can, whereas the
latter cannot, have independent checks upon his memory impressions, that is, checks whose evidential value
can be established without appeal to one's own memory
impressions. It is because he can avoid this sort of reliance upon his own memory that a public-language
speaker can distinguish between objective and subjective
reality—that he can distinguish between his memory impressions' seeming correct and their being correct, that
there is a distinction between how things seem to him
to be and how things are. He can do this because he

can utilize the testimony of other persons as a check
upon his own memory impressions. With regard to a
PL_1-speaker, however, it is because he cannot avoid this
sort of reliance upon his own memory that he cannot
distinguish between objective and subjective reality—
that he cannot distinguish between his memory impressions' seeming correct and their being correct, that there
is no distinction between how things seem to him to be
and how things are. He cannot do this because he cannot utilize the testimony of other persons as a check
upon his own memory impressions (of private experiential data). It is for this reason that it is a remarkable
difference between PL_1 and public language that speakers of the former but not the latter must rely in this
way upon their own memories when checking upon their
memory impressions. It is because he can avoid this sort
of reliance upon his own memory that the checking process of a public-language speaker is legitimate, and it is
because a PL_1-speaker cannot avoid this sort of reliance
upon his own memory that his checking process is illegitimate. The PL_1-speaker cannot possibly break out of
the sphere of his own memory impressions and check
them against something independent. It is this that sets
his putative language apart from public language, and
it is this that makes it impossible."

T: "I am surprised that you should think that this
meets my criticism. Once again I must tell you that
although you continue to *claim* that nonindependent
checks are not really checks, you have not shown this.
You merely reiterate the same old similarities and differences between PL_1 and public language upon which
we have for some time been in agreement, and then you
blithely insist that in light of their differences and despite their similarities the former language, in contrast

to the latter, must be seen to be impossible. But this I do not see. Why not? To answer this question, I, too, must rehearse old ground. PL_1 and public language, we have agreed, are similar in that a checking process will serve its purpose only to the extent that one's unchecked memory impressions (which entitle one to accept the existence of the unchecked checks that lie at checking's end) are correct. It is for this reason, I maintain, that it doesn't matter that testimony has an a priori evidential value for a public-language speaker. If he incorrectly remembers the various pieces of testimony, and so forth, that constitute his unchecked checks, his checking process will not be effective. So he must simply trust these unchecked memory impressions: the effective use of all else in the checking process depends upon them. If this is legitimate, and surely it is, then so is it legitimate for a PL_1-speaker to rest the evidential value of his checks upon his unchecked memory impressions: conversely, if the latter is not legitimate and a PL_1 is therefore impossible, then so is the former illegitimate and a public language is therefore impossible. I grant you that you, as a public-language speaker, have an independent factor involved in your checking process that I, as a PL_1-speaker, do not: most fundamentally, you can employ the testimony of others, and I cannot. But I deny that this constitutes a significant difference between our languages in virtue of which you can, as you put it, 'break out of the sphere of . . . [your] own memory impressions,' and I cannot. For the effectiveness of any checks you employ—the epistemic worth of your checking process—depends entirely on the use you make of those checks. And the use you make of them depends entirely upon the unchecked checks that lie at the end of your checking process and hence upon your unchecked memory impressions. Thus, the effectiveness of any

checks you employ—the epistemic worth of your checking process—depends entirely upon your unchecked
memory impressions. But this is precisely the case with
me as well: the effectiveness of my checks—the epistemic
worth of my checking process—also depends entirely
upon my unchecked memory impressions. Therefore, it
would be arbitrary to say that you can, and I cannot,
'break out of the sphere of . . . [one's] own memory
impressions.' Or if you do choose to say this in order
to emphasize the fact that you can and I cannot employ
independent checks, it would surely be arbitrary to go
on to add, as you do, that for this reason PL$_1$—in contrast to public language—must be impossible."

W: "I do not see that it is arbitrary to maintain the
impossibility of a PL$_1$ on the ground that this alleged
language has no room for a distinction between objective and subjective reality. Surely you must admit that
if you can have no way of distinguishing between the
actual history of your sensations (or any other of your
private experiential data) and your impression of this
history, then your PL$_1$-diary (or any other discourse in
a PL$_1$) is an impossibility. And it is my contention that
you cannot make this distinction between objective and
subjective reality because you are committed to accept
your own memory as 'the highest court of appeal' (*Inv.*,
56): as you are the first to confess, you can have no independent checks upon your memory impressions.
Hence, you cannot distinguish between your memory
impressions' seeming correct and their being correct, between how things are and how they seem to you to be.
Shoemaker puts the point that I wish to make as follows:

> Perhaps it will be said that I can know that one of
> my memories is mistaken by seeing that it conflicts

with the rest of my memories. But how is it that memories can 'conflict'? If I seem to remember seeing that a certain lot was vacant the day before yesterday, and also seem to remember seeing a tall building on that lot yesterday, I shall conclude that one or the other of my memories must be mistaken. But it is not that these memories are in themselves inconsistent. They 'conflict,' but what this means is that the conjunction of them is incompatible with a general truth I know about the world, namely that tall buildings cannot be built in a day. But could *my own* past experience, or rather my present memory of it, be sufficient to give me the general knowledge of the world, of causal laws and so on, that I would need in order to be able to conclude from what I seem to remember that one of my memories is false? I think not. If I am trying to make generalizations on the basis of my past experience as I remember it, but am not trying to make these generalizations consistent with the experience of other persons as well as with my own, there is no reason why I cannot make these generalizations complicated enough to be consistent with all my memories. To be sure, if I try to make my generalizations fairly simple, I shall probably find it impossible to make them consistent with all my memories. But suppose that I have formulated a set of relatively simple generalizations that are consistent with a majority of my memories, but inconsistent with a small minority of them. Can I conclude that the recalcitrant memories are false? Is it not possible that I could formulate a different set of generalizations, equally simple, that would 'save' an equally large but different set of my memories, so that memories that would be 'false' according to the first set of generalizations would be 'true' according to the second set, and vice versa? Just as the concept of a true account of reality, of how things are and have been, is different from the concept of how things seem *to me* to be and to have been, so also it is different from the concept of the simplest account consistent with most of *my* experiences, or with most of *my* memories. Yet the latter is just what my concept of reality would have to be if I could be entitled, without yet regarding what others say as relevant to the question of how things are and have been, to declare that certain of my memories are false because of other memories that I have, i.e., because they are incompatible with the simplest account that saves most of my memories." [22]

T: "I grant you that I am, as you say, committed to accept my own memory as 'the highest court of appeal' in that I can have no independent checks upon my memory impressions. I grant you, as well, that if my PL_1 left no room for a distinction between objective and subjective reality, then it would, indeed, be an impossible language. I think, however, that my language does have room for such a distinction, and I now propose to argue that you are mistaken in thinking that it follows from the admitted fact that I can have no independent checks that no such distinction is available to me. I propose, therefore, to address myself to Shoemaker's argument that you offer in behalf of this contention of yours.

"Shoemaker talks as though he would affirm:

(A) The concept of a true account of reality for a public-language speaker is the concept of the simplest account consistent with most of *our* experiences, or with most of *our* memories ('our' meaning those of the public, of people at large), whereas the concept of a true account of reality for a PL_1-speaker is the concept of the simplest account consistent with most of *my* experiences, or with most of *my* memories.

This sort of talk is open to the objection that even a public-language speaker's concept of a true account of

[22] Shoemaker, *op. cit.*, pp. 253–54.

reality cannot properly be identified with the concept of the simplest account consistent with most of our experiences or memories, since the simplest account does not always turn out to be the true account and since later generations often uncover the mistakes of earlier generations. Indeed, it could be objected, it will not do, either, to identify a public-language speaker's concept of a true account of reality with the concept of the simplest account consistent with most people's experiences or memories throughout all time. This will not do not only because the simplest account need not be the true one but also because it makes sense to suppose that everyone will, in fact, always be mistaken regarding one matter or another, even though it makes no sense to suppose that everyone will always be mistaken regarding everything or most things. Further, there need not be any one account that is *the* simplest account consistent with most people's experiences or memories. Shoemaker correctly notes that a person who does not (or cannot) avail himself of the testimony of others might formulate several equally simple accounts each of which would 'save' an equally large but different set of his memories. Similarly, a public-language speaker might formulate several equally simple accounts, each of which is consistent with most people's experiences or memories.

"For these reasons it would be a mistake to suppose that a public-language speaker's concept of a true account of reality is such that things must actually be as they are depicted to be by a particular (e.g., 'the simplest') account of them that is consistent with most people's experiences or memories, just as it would be a mistake to suppose that a PL_1-speaker's concept of a true account of reality is such that things must actually be as they are depicted to be by a particular (e.g., 'the simplest') account of them that is consistent with most of his experiences or memories. So if this is the position that Shoemaker meant to take, in talking as though he would affirm (A), then he is mistaken. We can, however, understand Shoemaker to mean something different by (A), and something that is quite true. It is true that a public-language speaker's concept of a true account of reality is the concept of an account whose acceptability (i.e., credibility or likelihood) is to be determined in accordance with the tests of its simplicity and its consistency with most people's experiences or memories. And it is true that a PL_1-speaker's concept of a true account of reality is the concept of an account whose acceptability is to be determined in accordance with the tests of its simplicity and its consistency with most of his experiences or memories. If it is these two truths that Shoemaker meant to bring out in writing as though he wished to say what I have formulated in (A), then I am quite prepared to accept (A) in this sense of (A). And from now on I shall assume that Shoemaker, too, would accept (A) as true in this sense of (A).

"In light of the foregoing considerations, I take it that Shoemaker's argument against the idea of a PL_1 could be put as follows. A public-language speaker can check his memory impressions against the memory impressions of others. By means of the tests of its simplicity and its consistency with the memory impressions of others and of himself, he can determine the acceptability of an account of the past, for example, an account of his own past sensations. He can in this way determine (i.e., be justified in believing) that one of his memory impressions is mistaken and that another is correct. Thus, he can distinguish between subjective reality and objective reality—between his merely seeming to remember a sensation and his correctly remembering a sensation, between his impression of the history of his sensations and the actual history of his sensations. In contrast, it will be said, a PL_1-speaker cannot check his memory impressions against the memory impressions of others. So he cannot determine the acceptability of an account of his own past sensations by means of the tests of its simplicity and its consistency with the memory impressions of *others and* of himself. He cannot in this way determine that one of his memory impressions is mistaken and that another is correct. Thus, he cannot distinguish between subjective reality and objective reality—between his merely seeming to remember a sensation and his correctly remembering a sensation, between his impression of the history of his sensations and the actual history of his sensations. Hence, his PL_1-diary, or any other discourse in a PL_1, is an impossibility.

"In reply, I admit that a PL_1-speaker cannot distinguish subjective reality from objective reality in the way that a public-language speaker can: as you say, he cannot, although a public-language speaker can, check his memory impressions against the memory impressions of others. But it does not follow from this that a PL_1-speaker cannot distinguish subjective reality from objective reality. It follows only that he cannot do this in the same way that a public-language speaker can do it. And this, after all, is only to be expected. For it is *logically* (conceptually) true that a public-language speaker can, and a PL_1-speaker cannot, check his memory impressions against the memory impressions of other persons. The meaning of 'public language' is such that a public-language speaker can do this. And, since we are assuming for purposes of our present discussion that a PL_1 is necessarily a PL_2, the meaning of 'PL_1' is such that a PL_1-speaker cannot do this.

"But if it is a priori true that this sort of checking is impossible for a PL_1-speaker, then surely it is strange to think it necessary that he should be able to employ such checks. He cannot employ them, and that is that. But you are mistaken to think that he therefore cannot employ any other checks. He can. He can check his memory impressions against other of his memory impressions. This, you will say, is not really to check them. But why not? You will say that this alleged way of checking leaves no room for a distinction between subjective and objective reality, that is, for a distinction between the actual history of his sensations and his impression of this history. This, however, is untrue. He can determine the acceptability of an account of his past sensations by means of the tests of its simplicity and its consistency with his own memory impressions. It is in this way that he will distinguish between his merely seeming to remember a sensation and his correctly remembering a sensation, that he will determine that one of his memory impressions is mistaken and that another is correct. If it is legitimate for a public-language speaker to use the *coherence* of memories (his own and others)— that is, the tests of the simplicity of an account and the consistency of the account with most people's memories—in order to determine the actual history of his sensations, then why is it illegitimate for a PL_1-speaker to use the *coherence* of memories (his own and not others)—that is, the tests of the simplicity of an account and the consistency of the account with most of his memories—in order to determine the actual history of his sensations? Both employ coherence as a method of determining the nature of the past, as a method of distinguishing the objective past from a subjective past. They differ in that one employs public coherence and the other private coherence. But you cannot say that the PL_1-speaker lacks a method for distinguishing the objective past from a subjective past. At most you can say that he does this in a private way, by means of private coherence, rather than in a public way, by means of public coherence. But then why should you expect anything else when he speaks a private language, in this case, a language that is both a PL_1 and a PL_2? Your criticism rests upon the claim that the PL_1-speaker cannot distinguish between objective and subjective reality. I have shown that he can. He does not make this distinction in the way that a public-language speaker makes it. But this is to be expected. It does not follow from this that he does not make this distinction. As I have shown, he does."

W: "As Aune has said:

> . . . as the word 'knowledge' is normally used—in everyday life and in scientific investigation—it is entirely possible for a person, perhaps a madman, to have perfectly coherent but perfectly erroneous ideas about himself, his surroundings, or anything else. The mere fact, in other words, that one's ideas are coherent is obviously no guarantee that those ideas exemplify knowledge.[23]

In light of our earlier discussion of the testimony thesis, it may well be that 'perfectly erroneous' is too strong a phrase, for we would allow that a person speaks a language, and in this sense has ideas, only if not too many of his ideas were erroneous. But, with this qualification, the general point is sound: the mere fact that one's ideas, or memory impressions, are coherent with one another will not enable one to distinguish between objective and subjective reality. One might, for example,

[23] B. Aune, "Feelings, Moods, and Introspection," *Mind*, LXXII (April, 1963), 191.

be under the illusion that one is Napoleon and one might be possessed of a coherent set of memory impressions to this effect. The mere coherence of one man's memories alone cannot suffice to distinguish the real past from an apparent past. It was for this reason that Wittgenstein enjoined us: 'Always get rid of the idea of the private object in this way: assume that it constantly changes, but that you do not notice the change because your memory constantly deceives you' (*Inv.*, p. 207). It is for this reason, too, that one's own memory cannot always be 'the highest court of appeal' (*Inv.*, 56).

"Thus, you are mistaken in thinking that a PL₁-speaker can distinguish objective from subjective reality but that he does it in a different way from that of a public-language speaker. He cannot make this distinction at all. He has no way of making it. You speak of his using a private method, a method of private coherence. But this is no method at all. For the concept of an objective past is not the concept of how the past seems to *me* to be. Yet this is what it would have to be if the method of determining the nature of the past were to be the 'private method' you advance. You rightly say that it is *logically* true that a public-language speaker can, and a PL₁-speaker cannot, check his memory impressions against the memory impressions of other persons. But you fail to understand the proper significance of this fact. It does not mean, as you seem to think, that such independent checks, being impossible for a PL₁-speaker, are therefore quite unnecessary so that his nonindependent checks must be viewed as legitimate after all. It means that, as a matter of logic, he cannot have the one thing that would enable him genuinely to check upon his memory impressions: thus, rather than saving him, logic reduces his position, the idea of his PL₁, to absurdity."

T: "Once again it comes clear that we remain upon old ground: the issue between us remains one wherein I maintain, and you deny, the legitimacy of nonindependent checks. You say that the mere coherence of one man's memories alone cannot suffice to distinguish the real past from an apparent past. If you mean that this coherence will not logically guarantee that the past is of a certain sort, doubtless you are correct. But then no such guarantee is provided by public coherence either. For, as I argued in first discussing Shoemaker's argument, it would be a mistake to suppose that a public-language speaker's concept of a true account of reality is such that things must actually be as they are depicted to be by a particular (e.g., 'the simplest') account of them that is consistent with most people's experiences or memories, just as it would be a mistake to suppose that a PL_1-speaker's concept of a true account of reality is such that things must actually be as they are depicted to be by a particular (e.g., 'the simplest') account of them that is consistent with most of his experiences or memories. If, on the other hand, you mean that the mere coherence of one man's memories alone will not serve him as a means by which he can determine the acceptability of an account of the past, that is, as a method by means of which he can be justified in accepting statements about the past, then you beg the question at issue: you simply reiterate that his private method is not really a method at all.

"You point to the truth that a man might be under the illusion that he is Napoleon and might be possessed of a set of coherent memories to this effect. This does bring out the fact that, as I have just said, private coherence will not logically guarantee the truth of one's account of the past—any more than public coherence will provide such a guarantee. You wish, however, to use this truth to show that the mere coherence of one man's memories alone cannot suffice to distinguish the real past from an apparent past in the sense that this private coherence will not serve him as a means by which he can determine the acceptability of an account of the past, that is, as a method by means of which he can be justified in accepting statements about the past. But this it will not show. Of course, it may not help the poor man of your example to call up additional memories: these may only confirm him in his Napoleonic delusion. On the other hand, this may help him: he may regain his sanity, rid himself of his delusion, and correctly remember his past. Similarly, it may not help this poor man to consult the testimony of other persons: this, too, may only confirm him in his Napoleonic delusion. For he may remain insane, and he may seem to remember all manner of (actually nonexistent) testimony that only confirms him in his delusion. Similarly, too, this may help him: he may regain his sanity, rid himself of his delusion, and correctly remember his past. The crucial thing to be noticed here is that the testimony of others will serve this man as an effective check upon his memory impressions only to the extent that his memory impressions of the testimony are correct. Thus, this example will not show that private coherence, in contrast with public coherence, leaves no room for a distinction between subjective and objective reality. Rather, it serves to reveal the fact that there is no better reason to say that public coherence is a legitimate method of determining the acceptability of an account of the past than there is to say this of private coherence. It brings out the fact that even though the method of public coherence, unlike the method of private coherence, enables one to employ the testimony of others as a check upon one's memory impressions, one's use of this testimony can be no more effective than one's unchecked memory impressions of this testimony. Thus, there is no better reason to affirm the legitimacy of the independent checks of a public-language speaker than there is to affirm the legitimacy of the nonindependent checks of a PL_1-speaker.

"You suggest that I get rid of the private object by assuming that it constantly changes but that I do not notice the change because my memory constantly deceives me. But a person cannot sensibly repudiate the general trustworthiness of his own memory. It would therefore be absurd for me to make the assumption that you suggest, just as it would be absurd for a public-language speaker to make this assumption regarding his memory of public objects. Neither a PL_1-speaker nor a public-language speaker can have any way of telling that his memory constantly deceives him: one can check upon this or that particular memory, but no one can check upon his whole set of memories. We must all of us assume that our memories are generally trustworthy if we are to talk sense.

"You say that the concept of an objective past is not the concept of how the past seems *to me* to be, and that this is what it would have to be if the method of determining the nature of the past were to be the 'private method' that I advance. But this is to overlook the logical differences between public language and PL_1, assuming, as we are, that a PL_1 is necessarily a PL_2. As you say, the concept of an objective past is not the concept of how the past seems *to me* to be, *if,* that is, we are speaking of a public-language speaker's concept of the past: his is a concept of an objective past such that the nature of this objective past is to be ascertained (i.e., the acceptability of an account of it is to be determined) by means of the tests of the simplicity of an account and its consistency with the memory impressions of *others and* himself. If, however, we are speaking of a PL_1-speaker's concept of the past, then the concept of an objective past is the concept of how the past seems *to me* to be: his is a concept of an objective past such that the nature of the objective past is to be ascertained (i.e., the acceptability of an account of it is to be determined) by means of the tests of the simplicity of an account and its consistency with *his own* memory impressions.

"Rather than say that you overlook these logical differences between public language and PL_1, it would be more accurate to say that you make arbitrary use of them. I mean that although you notice these differences and, indeed, insist upon them, you do so because you wish to insist that a PL_1 must be faulty (impossible) in that it is logically different from public language. You say that since, as a matter of logic, a PL_1-speaker cannot utilize the testimony of others and so cannot have independent checks upon his memory impressions, logic reduces the idea of his PL_1 to absurdity. But it is arbitrary of you to insist that a PL_1 is impossible simply because its logic is different from that of public language. This would not, I admit, be arbitrary had you succeeded in showing that the idea of a PL_1 has no room for a distinction between objective reality and subjective reality. But this you have not done.[24]

"We have seen that both public language and PL_1 involve the use of coherence tests to distinguish the real past from an apparent past. We have seen that they differ in that the former employs public coherence and

[24] Cf. J. N. Findlay, review of *Philosophical Investigations*, *Philosophy*, XXX (April, 1955), 176–78; C. L. Hardin, "Wittgenstein on Private Languages," *Journal of Philosophy*, LVI (June 4, 1959); B. Medlin, "Critical Notice" of A. J. Ayer's *The Concept of a Person and Other Essays*, *Australasian Journal of Philosophy*, XLII (Dec., 1964), 416–17.

the latter private coherence. You have emphasized the difference between the two sorts of language, saying that only a public-language speaker can break out of the sphere of his own memory impressions. I have granted this difference when this is taken to mean that only a public-language speaker can have independent checks upon his memory impressions. I have emphasized the similarity between the two sorts of language, saying that the effectiveness, or epistemic worth, of a person's checking process—be that person a public-language speaker or a PL_1-speaker—is entirely dependent upon one's own unchecked memory impressions. You have granted this similarity when this is taken to mean that the use to which one puts one's checks depends entirely upon one's unchecked memory impressions, which is not to deny that, unlike a PL_1-speaker, a public-language speaker can have independent checks upon his memory impressions. We agree upon these things, and yet we tend to emphasize different things among those upon which we agree. Why? You emphasize the admitted difference between public language and PL_1 because on the basis of this difference you declare that PL_1, unlike public language, has no room for a distinction between objective and subjective reality and is therefore impossible. I emphasize the admitted similarity between public language and PL_1 because on the basis of this similarity I maintain that PL_1, like public language, has room for a distinction between objective and subjective reality and so is not, therefore, impossible.

"How are we to settle the ultimate disagreement between us? It would appear that we cannot do so. We disagree over the question: Is it the case that PL_1, unlike public language, has no room for a distinction between objective and subjective reality and is therefore impossible? We agree on all of the factors to which each of us appeals in support of his answer to this question. We disagree only with regard to the proper answer to this question in the light of the factors that we have adduced and upon which we agree. It seems to me that you are being arbitrary when you answer this question in the affirmative, for I think that you put insufficient weight upon the admitted similarity between public language and PL_1. But, then, I am sure that you think it equally arbitrary of me to answer the question in the negative, for you think that I fail to attach the proper importance to the admitted difference between public language and PL_1. It seems to me that you are unduly intolerant when you repudiate the idea of a PL_1 on the ground that it does not conform to the logic of public language. But, then, I'm sure that you find me to be insufficiently discriminating when I embrace the idea of a PL_1 despite its departure from the logic of public language."

W: "Ironically, upon this at least we can agree: that there does seem to be no way to settle this ultimate disagreement between us."

9) Summary and Prospectus

On this strange note of agreement, let us temporarily suspend our imaginary debate between the Wittgensteinian and the traditionist. For purposes of this stage of the debate it has been assumed that a PL_1 is unserviceable, that is, that it is necessarily a PL_2. Both parties to the discussion have agreed that it follows from this assumption that a traditionist cannot have independent checks upon his memory impressions of his private experiential data.

They have, likewise, agreed that if the nonindependent checks of the traditionist are illegitimate then he cannot distinguish between subjective and objective reality—between his memory impressions only seeming correct and their being correct, between his only seeming to follow the rules of a PL_1 and his actually following its rules. Thus, they have agreed that if the nonindependent checks of the traditionist are illegitimate, then a PL_1 is impossible. Their essential disagreement is over the legitimacy or illegitimacy of the traditionist's nonindependent checks upon his memory impressions. The traditionist affirms, and the Wittgensteinian denies, that these are genuine checks, that is, checks that will enable one to distinguish objective reality from subjective reality.

Neither of our disputants has been able to convince the other that he is mistaken in this their fundamental area of disagreement, despite the fact that each accepts the facts upon which the other bases his thesis. This leads us now to suggest that their differences may comprise not so much a matter of logical fact as a matter of linguistic or logical preference or decision. The Wittgensteinian demands independent checkability for claims about the past occurrence of one's own experiential data; the traditionist allows that nonindependent checkability will suffice. Perhaps this is a dispute that could be resolved only by a change of attitude and not by the cold light of reason. At any rate, we see no way to settle this portion of the debate between the Wittgensteinian and the traditionist.

On the other hand, we have not yet seen the last of this, the first prong of the internal attack upon the private object. In Chapter IV we shall have to consider an assault upon the private object that is an amalgam of the first and second prongs of the internal attack. It therefore remains to be seen whether this first prong of the internal attack, which has so far failed to achieve undisputed success, can so succeed when it is used in fresh arguments in which it is combined with the second prong of the internal attack. First, however, we shall consider by itself, in Chapter III, the second prong of the internal attack, namely, the external attack upon the private object.

III |
The External Attack

1) Prologue

We turn now to an examination of the external attack upon PL_1 or, otherwise stated, upon the notion of the private object. As we have indicated (cf. Ch. I, Sec. 4), this is the Wittgensteinian attempt to prove that a PL_1 is unserviceable, that is, that it is not a possible base for a common language and shared knowledge. Alternatively speaking, it is the attempt to prove that a PL_1 is necessarily a PL_2. Should the external assault fail, then the internal assault will have failed also, and the traditionist will be victorious, for the external attack is the second prong of the internal attack. (However, in this case, it would be too strong to claim *complete* victory for the traditionist: to undermine the Wittgensteinian arguments against his position is one thing, to establish the correctness of his position is another. Still, to accomplish the former would be to perform an important feat and one that is essential to the achievement of the latter.) If, on the other hand, the external assault should succeed, then either the first prong of the internal assault also succeeds (in which case traditionism will have been vanquished) or the first prong of the internal assault fails (in which case each side in the controversy must content itself with partial victory and partial defeat).

In Chapter I, we employed the following three renditions of the proposition that the Wittgensteinian hopes to support by means of the external attack, the first two being in the formal mode and the third in the material mode:

(1) A PL_1 is necessarily a PL_2.
(2) A PL_1 is unserviceable.
(3) Private objects are unserviceable.

Yet another way in which we may render this proposition, this rendition also being in the material mode, is:

(4) No one (logically) can know of the private objects of another.

In the course of our future discussion, we shall also have occasion to employ variants of the following version of this proposition that although less exact than (4) is also more familiar than any of (1)–(4).

(5) No one (logically) can know the mind of another.

2) *The Contradiction Argument*

One of the arguments that Wittgensteinians sometimes use in conducting the external attack upon PL_1 is what we shall call the *contradiction argument*. The traditionist typically claims that the base of our ordinary, common language is a PL_1', a PL_1 that one learns from one's own case by associating linguistic terms with one's own experiential data (cf. Ch. I, Sec. 2). In particular, he claims that one is able to know about and talk about the experiential data of others because one learns the meanings of terms that refer to experiential data by attending to one's own experiential data, one's own private objects. "What is attacked [by Wittgenstein] is the assumption that once I know from my *own* case what pain, tickling, or consciousness is, then I can transfer the ideas of these things to objects outside myself ([*Inv.*] 283)." [1]

In opposing this traditionist claim, Wittgenstein has said:

> If one has to imagine someone else's pain on the model of one's own, this is none too easy a thing to do: for I have to imagine pain which I *do not feel* on the model of the pain which I *do feel*. That is, what I have to do is not simply to make a transition in imagination from one place of pain to another. As, from pain in the hand to pain in the arm. For I am not to

[1] N. Malcolm, "Wittgenstein's *Philosophical Investigations*," *Knowledge and Certainty: Essays and Lectures* (Englewood Cliffs, N.J.: Prentice-Hall, Inc., 1963), p. 105.

imagine that I feel pain in some region of his body. (Which would also be possible.) (*Inv.*, 302)

These remarks of Wittgenstein's may be given the following interpretation, and it is this interpretation that we refer to as the *contradiction argument:*

(1) According to the traditionalist, I learn what "pain" means by attending to my own pains.

(2) Any pains that I feel are pains that are necessarily mine.[2]

(3) Hence, the traditionist must admit that I learn what "pain" means by attending to pains that are necessarily mine.

(4) It follows that part of the meaning of "pain" for the traditionist is that its referents are mine.

(5) For the traditionist, then, "pain" means (is short for) "my pain."

(6) In this case, it would be meaningless (or contradictory) to speak of another's pain.

---

[2] In light of Plantinga's interesting discussion of the contradiction argument in A. Plantinga, "Things and Persons," *Review of Metaphysics* XIV (March, 1961), 517–19, it is especially important to specify the meaning of "pains that are necessarily (of necessity) mine." To say of a pain that it is necessarily mine is *not* to say that it is necessarily true that the pain occurred. It is to say that although it is a contingent fact that the pain occurred, it is a necessary truth that no one other than myself has that pain. From this necessary truth it follows that I do not share this particular pain with anyone else and that had I not had it, it would not have occurred (so that even if I had not had it, no one else would have had it). An important Wittgensteinian reason for accepting (2) as a conceptual truth is that it is essential to the notion of an identifying description of a particular pain that the pain be describable as the pain of one particular person. Cf. P. F. Strawson, *Individuals: An Essay in Descriptive Metaphysics* (London: Methuen and Co. Ltd., 1959), pp. 40–44, 97.

(7) The traditionist must therefore admit that one cannot speak of or know of the pains of another.

(8) Since pain has been used simply as an example of
an experiential datum, the point, generally stated, is
that a PL_1' is necessarily a PL_2: on the traditionist
position, no one could know the mind of another,
and so no one could understand the experiential
language of another.

The traditionist, however, may reply as follows: "Although (1)–(3) are true, the argument is invalid. None
of (4)–(8) follows from (1)–(3), and I may therefore embrace the position expressed by (1)–(3) without allowing
the truth of any of (4)–(8). Although the pains to which
I attend in learning the meaning of 'pain' are pains that
are necessarily mine, the meaning that I give to 'pain' is
not such that pains, of necessity, belong to me. I intend
'pain' to refer to items of the sort I am attending to,
except that they are *either* mine (and necessarily mine)
or someone else's (and necessarily his). The significance
of the 'except . . .' rider consists partly in this: I so
use 'pain' that, by definition, (a) no pain particulars are
shared (by two or more persons), and (b) no pain particular that in fact is felt by one person might instead
have been felt by another."

Now it seems to us that the traditionist's rebuttal is
effective. When the external attack is couched in the form
of the contradiction argument, it fails for just the
reasons that the traditionist has offered. That is, the
argument is invalid: none of (4)–(8) follows from (1)–(3).
This is not, however, to grant the correctness of the
traditionist's claim that he can meaningfully speak of
his own and of others' pains. Whether or not he can do
so remains to be seen. Whether the external attack can

succeed when it is conceived in a different way is what we shall now go on to consider. For, as we have said, the contradiction argument is only one interpretation of the foregoing remarks of Wittgenstein's. We shall next devote considerable attention to another interpretation of those remarks, an interpretation that seems to us to constitute a very powerful version of the external attack.

Before dealing with this, it is worth noting that Malcolm, who once accepted the former version of the external attack as both successful and true to Wittgenstein's intentions, has since rejected it as being neither of these.[3] He has gone on to replace this interpretation of Wittgenstein's remarks with the version of the external attack that we are about to discuss. Malcolm's reason for rejecting the former is his acceptance of the Wittgensteinian dictum: "In so far as it makes *sense* to say that my pain is the same as his, it is also possible for us both to have the same pain." [4] The idea is that it makes sense to say of two people that they do or do not feel the same pain particular only if it is possible that they both do feel it. Since this is impossible, it is concluded that such talk is nonsense and that (2) and (3) are therefore nonsense. This line of thought seems to us mistaken, however. It makes perfectly good sense to assert conceptual truths, and this is what one does when one asserts that it is not the case that my pain is (numerically) the

[3] Cf. Malcolm, "Wittgenstein's *Philosophical Investigations*," *op. cit.*, pp. 105–6 and n. 2 on pp. 105–6. The former interpretation of Wittgenstein's remarks was also accepted and employed by B. Aune, "The Problem of Other Minds," *Philosophical Review*, LXX (July, 1961), 324–25, 336.

[4] *Inv.*, 253. Cf. *Inv.*, 246–52, 398; G. E. Moore, "Wittgenstein's Lectures in 1930–33," *Philosophical Papers* (London: George Allen and Unwin Ltd., 1959), pp. 306–12; M. Black, *A Companion to Wittgenstein's "Tractatus"* (Ithaca, N.Y.: Cornell University Press, 1964), pp. 309–10.

same as his. Such conceptual truths are, in Wittgenstein's terms, contributions to the "grammar" of the language, and, as such, there seems little reason to call them *senseless*.

3) The Direct-Evidence Argument

Wittgenstein's remarks in *Inv.*, 302 (quoted above) may also be understood as an expression of what we shall call the *direct-evidence argument*. Malcolm puts it this way:

> A more correct account of Wittgenstein's point in sec. 302 is the following: A proponent of the privacy of sensations rejects circumstances and behavior as a criterion of the sensations of others, this being essential to his viewpoint. He does not need (and could not have) a criterion for the existence of pain that he feels. But surely he will need a criterion for the existence of pain that *he* does *not* feel. Yet he cannot have one and still hold to the privacy of sensation. If he sticks to the latter, he ought to admit that he has not the faintest idea of what would count for or against the occurrence of sensations that he does not feel. His conclusion should be not that it is a contradiction, but that it is unintelligible to speak of the sensations of others.[5]

On this view, for the traditionist to conceive of someone else's pain on the model of his own "is none too easy a thing to do" (*Inv.*, 302) in that ". . . he does not understand the sentence 'That human figure has feelings'

[5] "Wittgenstein's *Philosophical Investigations*," *op. cit.*, p. 105, n. 2.

. . ." [6] Indeed, more fully articulated, the point is not only that he cannot understand talk about the feelings or sensations of others, but that he cannot conceive of (or understand talk about) *any* experiential data of other persons.

> "That there should be thinking or pain other than my own is unintelligible," he ought to hold. This would be a rigorous solipsism, and a correct outcome of the assumption that one can know only from one's own case what the mental phenomena are. An equivalent way of putting it would be: "When I say 'I am in pain,' by 'pain' I mean a certain inward state. When I say '*He* is in pain,' by 'pain' I mean *behavior*. I cannot attribute pain to others *in the same sense* that I attribute it to myself." [7]

This line of attack upon the traditionist is not the exclusive property of Malcolm and the later Wittgenstein. It was adumbrated by the early Wittgenstein:

> For what the solipsist *means* is quite correct; only it cannot be *said*, but makes itself manifest.
> The world is *my* world: this is manifest in the fact that the limits of *language* (of that language which alone I understand) mean the limits of *my* world. [8]

It was given a positivistic expression by Carnap:

> All that S_2 can verify when he asserts "S_1 is thirsty" is that S_1's body is in such and such a state, and a

---

[6] Malcolm, "Knowledge of Other Minds," *Knowledge and Certainty, op. cit.,* p. 131.

[7] *Ibid.,* p. 137.

[8] *Tractatus Logico-Philosophicus,* D. F. Pears and B. F. McGuinness, trans. (London: Routledge and Kegan Paul, 1961). Sec. 5.62.

statement asserts no more than can be verified. If by "the thirst of S_1" we understand not the physical state of his body but his sensations of thirst, i.e., something nonmaterial, then S_1's thirst is fundamentally beyond the reach of S_2's recognition.

A statement about S_1's thirst would then be fundamentally unverifiable by S_2, it would be for him in principle impossible to understand, void of sense.

In general, every statement in any person's protocol language [i.e., experiential-datum language] would have sense for that person alone, would be fundamentally outside the understanding of other persons, without sense for them. Hence every person would have his own protocol language. Even when the same words and sentences occur in various protocol languages, their sense would be different, they could not even be compared. *Every protocol language could therefore be applied only solipsistically; there would be no intersubjective protocol language. This is the consequence obtained by consistent adherence to the usual view and terminology* (rejected by the author).[9]

And likewise by Ayer:

. . . just as I must define material things and my own self in terms of their empirical manifestations, so I must define other people in terms of their empirical manifestations—that is, in terms of the behaviour of their bodies, and ultimately in terms of [my] sense-contents. The assumption that "behind" these sense-contents there are entities which are not even in principle accessible to my observation can have no more

[9] R. Carnap, *The Unity of Science*, M. Black, trans., Psyche Miniatures, General Series No. 63 (London: Kegan Paul, Trench, Trubner, and Co. Ltd., 1934) pp. 79–80. Cf. R. Carnap, "Psychology in Physical Language," in A. J. Ayer, ed., *Logical Positivism* (Glencoe, Ill.: Free Press, 1959); B. Russell, *The Philosophy of Logical Atomism* in R. C. Marsh, ed., *Logic and Knowledge: Essays, 1901–1950* (London: George Allen and Unwin, 1956), p. 201.

significance for me than the admittedly metaphysical assumption that such entities "underlie" the sense-contents which constitute material things for me, or my own self. And thus I find that I have as good a reason to believe in the existence of other people as I have to believe in the existence of material things. For in each case my hypothesis is verified by the occurrence in my sense-history of the appropriate series of sense-contents.

It must not be thought that this reduction of other people's experiences to one's own in any way involves a denial of their reality. . . . If I know that an object behaves in every way as a conscious being must, by definition, behave, then I know that it is really conscious.[10]

3a) THE NOTION OF "CRITERION"

The direct-evidence argument hinges on the notion of a criterion. Wittgenstein and Malcolm use "criterion" in accordance with a number of the ordinary meanings of this word: for example, "a test, principle, rule, canon, or standard, by which anything is judged or estimated"; "a distinguishing mark or characteristic attaching to a thing, by which it can be judged or estimated" (*O.E.D.*). Difficulties often arise in connection with attempts to make clear the nature of the relationship between criteria and the uses of words. For example: criteria do not *entail* the applicability of an expression (cf. *Inv.*, 183), yet Malcolm has suggested that criteria can settle an issue beyond (all sensible) question;[11] criteria are tied to

---

[10] A. J. Ayer, *Language, Truth and Logic* (London: Victor Gollancz Ltd., 2nd ed., 1946), p. 130.
[11] "Wittgenstein's *Philosophical Investigations*," *op. cit.*, pp. 112–17, esp. p. 113.

certain circumstances (cf. *Inv.*, 160, 164), and they can conflict.[12]

Two notions that stand particularly close to "criteria" are "definition" and "evidence." Indeed, there are times when one may feel inclined to *identify* criteria with either definitions or evidence. A criterion (in the sense of a distinguishing mark) is not unlike evidence (in the sense of that which manifests or makes evident, a mark or sign); and a criterion is similar to a definition in that each tells us something about the meaning of words. Given these similarities, it seems appropriate to regard criteria as some kind of evidence when they are explicitly related to objects, states, occurrences, or processes (e.g., *Inv.*, 149, 159–60, 185, 692), and as affording a definition of sorts when they are explicitly related to word usage (e.g., *Inv.*, 190, 258, 354). But of course the difference between asking for the criteria of X and for the criteria of "X" is one of mode, not of substance, as it were.

The job of elucidating the exact intentions of Wittgenstein and Malcolm with respect to the meaning of "criterion" is notoriously difficult, and we shall not even attempt it here. It is, however, necessary for our present purposes to give some account of this notion.

We shall view criteria as a kind of evidence; indeed, we shall use the terms *direct evidence* and *criterion* synonymously. Criterial evidence for p is that which is evidence for p in virtue of the meaning of p, whereas symptomatic evidence (or, synonymously speaking, *indirect,* or inductive, evidence) for p is that which is evidence for p in virtue of our knowledge of empirical correlations. If X is a criterion of p, then it is logically necessary that X

[12] Cf. N. Malcolm, *Dreaming* (London: Routledge and Kegan Paul, 1959), Ch. VI.

is evidence for p; whereas, if X is a symptom of p, it is a matter of contingent empirical fact that X is evidence for p. Thus, the presence of a certain virus is criterial for the presence of virus pneumonia, while the presence of a fever is at best symptomatic; the look and feel of rain are direct evidence that it is raining, and the falling barometer provides only a symptom.[13]

3b) THE DIRECT-EVIDENCE PRINCIPLE

In developing the direct-evidence argument, the Wittgensteinian may appeal to what we shall call the *direct-evidence principle:* p meaningfully affirms the existence of a particular state of affairs only if it is possible to have direct evidence for p. In particular, we may interpret the above remarks of Malcolm's as constituting the following argument against traditionism: "We Wittgensteinians may speak meaningfully of the minds of other persons, but any putative statement, p, that is purportedly about the mind of another is meaningless when made by a traditionist. For traditionism holds that experiential data are private objects, entities that are conceptually independent of any publicly observable phenomena. Hence, whereas a Wittgensteinian treats the behavior and circumstances of others as direct evidence for p, this avenue is not open to traditionists. It follows that a traditionist cannot possibly obtain direct evidence regarding the mental states of others. To do so would require him to have another's thought, feel another's pain, and so forth. But this is impossible (or nonsense) since it would re-

[13] Cf. L. Wittgenstein, *The Blue and Brown Books* (Oxford: Basil Blackwell, 1958), pp. 24–5; *Inv.,* 354.

quire him to *be* another person. According to the direct-
evidence principle, then, we may conclude that a traditionist cannot meaningfully affirm p, and, *a fortiori*,
cannot know, or even conceive, of the mind of another."

The traditionist is not without his defenses, however,
as we see in the ensuing dialogue.

T: "Why should I accept the direct-evidence principle?
So long as I am able to obtain evidence of some kind
both for and against p, there is no reason to call p meaningless. In his above-quoted comments, Malcolm maintained that the traditionist 'ought to admit that he has
not the faintest idea of what would count for or against
the occurrence of sensations [or any experiential data]
that he does not feel [or experience].' But this is not so.
We traditionists may obtain evidence for or against p by
means of the traditional analogy argument regarding
other minds. This argument may take many forms,[14]
but in essence it comes to this: Time and again when
my body has been in a state, $\emptyset$, I have had an experiential datum, $\cancel{V}$. That (other) body is $\emptyset$. It follows with
probability that another person 'owns' that body and has
$\cancel{V}$: The bodily state $\emptyset$ is construed to include not only
the nature of the body and its behavior but also its
environmental conditions. The probability with which
the conclusion follows from the premises increases sig-
nificantly when the premises are expanded to include a
detailed description of the analogy between the states of
the two bodies over a lengthy time period: For example,

[14] For example, cf. A. J. Ayer, *The Problem of Knowledge*
(Harmondsworth: Penguin Books, 1956), Ch. V, Sec. vi; J. S.
Mill, *An Examination of Sir William Hamilton's Philosophy*,
6th ed. (New York: Longmans, Green, and Co., Inc., 1889),
pp. 243–44; H. H. Price, "Our Evidence for the Existence of
Other Minds," *Philosophy*, XIII (1938).

both bodies have often 'winced' when punctured; both bodies have often 'answered "Noon" ' at noon when stimulated by 'What's the time?' Therefore, although it is impossible that we have direct evidence for p, we may obtain indirect evidence for p. This is enough for the meaningfulness of p. We thereby repudiate the direct-evidence principle and the argument that rests upon it."

W: "You seem not to realize that an inductive argument such as yours, indeed, no argument, could ever afford probability to a meaningless 'conclusion.' As Malcolm says of Mill's version of this argument, 'If Mill has no criterion for the existence of feelings other than his own then in that sense he does not understand the sentence, "It is *probable* that that human figure has feelings." ' [15] Let me anticipate your response by quoting Malcolm, Wittgenstein, and then Malcolm again:

> There is a familiar inclination to make the following reply: 'Although I have no criterion of verification still I understand, for example, the sentence "He has a pain." For I understand the meaning of "I have a pain," and "He has a pain" means that he has the *same* thing I have when I have a pain.' But this is a fruitless maneuver. If I do not know how to establish that someone has a pain then I do not know how to establish that he has the *same* as I have when I have a pain.[16]

> It is as if I were to say: 'You surely know what "It is 5 o'clock here" means; so you also know what "It's 5 o'clock on the sun" means. It means simply that it is just the same time there as it is here when it is 5 o'clock.'—The explanation by means of *identity* does

---

[15] "Knowledge of Other Minds," *op. cit.*, p. 131. Cf. Ayer, *Language, Truth and Logic, op. cit.*, p. 129; Carnap, "Psychology in Physical Language," *op. cit.*, pp. 176–77, 179–80.
[16] "Knowledge of Other Minds," *op. cit.*, pp. 131–32.

not work here. For I know well enough that one can call 5 o'clock here and 5 o'clock there 'the same time,' but what I do not know is in what cases one is to speak of its being the same time here and there.

In exactly the same way it is no explanation to say: the supposition that he has a pain is simply the supposition that he has the same as I. For *that* part of the grammar is quite clear to me: that is, that one will say that the stove has the same experience as I, *if* one says: it is in pain and I am in pain.[17]

You cannot improve my understanding of 'He has a pain' by this recourse to the notion of 'the same,' unless you give me a criterion for saying that someone has the same as I have. If you can do this you will have no use for the argument from analogy: and if you cannot then you do not understand the supposed conclusion of that argument. A philosopher who purports to rely on the analogical argument cannot, I think, escape this dilemma." [18]

T: "I'm afraid that all of this quoting has accomplished little for you. Take some of Malcolm's words, for example: 'If I do not know how to establish that someone has a pain then I do not know how to establish that he has the *same* as I have when I have a pain.' Like the rest of the foregoing, it is either trivially true, and inconsequential, or it begs the question. If it means that if I can't get evidence (direct and/or indirect) for the one, then I can't get evidence (direct and/or indirect) for the other, then it is an ineffectual tautology. Alternatively, if it means that if I can't get direct evidence for p then p is meaningless, you argue in a circle. Apparently the latter is what is intended. But it will not do simply to reaffirm the direct-evidence principle by way of reply to my criticism of this principle. That you are doing this may

[17] *Inv.*, 350.
[18] "Knowledge of Other Minds," *op. cit.*, p. 132.

be made clear as follows: You claim that p is meaningless for me, citing the direct-evidence principle as your reason. I reject this principle, offering the analogy argument as my reason. You counter by saying that the analogy argument cannot work because, on the direct-evidence principle, its conclusion is meaningless. If you are to defeat my argument you must show that the analogy argument is unworkable on some ground other than the direct-evidence principle. We agree that it is impossible for me to have direct evidence for p. We disagree on whether p is then meaningless for me. You will not succeed in proving your side of this issue by insisting that you are correct. And this is what you do when you say that my reasons for holding p to be meaningful, namely, that I can provide indirect evidence for p, fail because p is meaningless (due to the impossibility of my having direct evidence). If you wish to avoid circularity, you must provide some other reason for your claim that the analogy argument fails to provide indirect evidence for p."

W: "Yes, I see your point, and I agree with it. It will not do for us to beg the question in the way you indicate. As you say, we must show in some noncircular fashion that the analogy argument is unworkable. First, however, I should like to note that the foregoing comments of Malcolm's and Wittgenstein's do make an important point when they are not used quite as I just attempted to use them. A traditionist might claim that simply because he understands 'I am in pain,' it must be that he understands 'He is in pain,' thinking, as Wittgenstein suggested, that it is enough to say that the latter ascribes to another the *same* as the former ascribes to oneself. But this is to ignore the legitimate requirement that syn-

thetic statements (i.e., factual or nonlogical statements)
be empirically testable."

T: "Right. Such a traditionist gambit would fail for the
reason you mention. We can talk about the world only if
our claims about the world may be checked by empirical
means. Thus, I would propose that we accept what I
call the *testability principle:* An utterance is a meaningful (synthetic) statement only if it is possible to have
(empirical) evidence for it and to have (empirical) evidence against it. (On the usual use of 'evidence,' one who
asserts, and is entitled to assert, that he is now in pain
does not do so on the basis of evidence, nor is it possible
(or sensible to say) that he then has evidence for the
truth of his statement; nevertheless, it must be possible
that other persons, or he himself at other times, have
evidence for the truth or falsity of his statement.) It is
my position that since the analogy argument enables a
traditionist to satisfy this principle with respect to statements about the minds of others, it should be allowed
that he may meaningfully make such statements."

3c) THE INDIRECT-EVIDENCE PRINCIPLE

W: "I join you in accepting the testability principle. I
must dissent, however, from your contention that the
traditionist's alleged statements about other minds do not
run afoul of this principle. If the analogy argument were
workable, then the traditionist's statements about other
minds would meet the standard set by the testability
principle. But this argument is not workable for the
following reason: To have indirect evidence for p, where

p affirms the existence of a particular state of affairs (e.g., that of a pitcher being in the cupboard, or of someone else having a toothache), one must have knowledge of an empirical correlation between states of the kind (A) referred to by p and states of some other kind (B). One's inductive (or indirect) evidence for p consists in one's knowledge of such a correlation together with one's knowledge of the existence of a certain B. One then infers that p, that is, one infers that another A stands to this B as the A's have stood to the B's in the known correlation. Now one could have indirect evidence for p only if one could have direct evidence for p. For unless states of kind A were such that we could have evidence for their existence independent of their empirical correlation with states of some other kind, we could never discover any such empirical correlations at all. Once we know of one such correlation, say that of A's and B's, we can obtain evidence for many more correlations between A's and other states, say C's, D's, and E's: this we can do by finding a correlation between B's and C's and between C's and D's and between D's and E's. But we could never know of the *initial* correlation between A's and B's if something did not, by *definition* of 'A,' count as evidence for the existence of A's: that is, we could not have indirect evidence for the existence of A's, if we could not have direct evidence for the existence of A's. I therefore affirm what I call the *indirect-evidence principle:* If it is impossible to have direct evidence for p (where p affirms the existence of a particular state of affairs), then it is impossible to have indirect evidence for p. You have admitted that a traditionist can have no direct evidence for his statements about the minds of others. You ought, then, also to admit that he can have no indirect evidence either. In this case, such would-be statements are meaningless since they violate the testability principle: they are susceptible neither of direct nor of indirect evidence." [19]

T: "I grant you that if the indirect-evidence principle were acceptable then, for just the reasons you mention, we traditionists could not speak of, or conceive of, other minds: in this case, it would have been proven that a PL_1 is unserviceable. It is therefore incumbent upon me to undermine this principle and to meet the argument that you have presented on its behalf. And this I will now attempt.

"You rightly point out that, on my position, it is impossible for one to obtain direct evidence for a statement about the mind of another. The only candidates for direct evidence are knowledge of the bodily states of another and (as it might seem to some) undergoing the experiences of another. But the former can't be direct evidence for a speaker of a PL_1, and the latter is contradictory. Nevertheless, I maintain that indirect evidence is obtainable, indeed, that such evidence is provided by the analogy argument. I contend that since I have often been in pain—while wincing or groaning after a tack has penetrated my foot—a similar state of another body makes it probable that there is another person, associated with that body, who also is in pain. And this is but a simple example of the use to which I may put the analogy argument: I also employ more complicated versions of the same technique to infer that someone else is in pain but trying not to show it, and so on.

"You will say, I am sure, that my argument fails utterly because the empirical correlation of which I have knowledge is, at best, a correlation between bodily states

[19] Cf. S. Shoemaker, *Self-Knowledge and Self-Identity* (Ithaca, N.Y.: Cornell University Press, 1963), pp. 165–68, *et passim*.

and *my* pains, whereas what is needed is knowledge of a correlation between bodily states and *his* pains (the pains of the 'owner' of that body). But this, as you well know, is, on traditionist principles, impossible: for it is a conceptual truth that one cannot feel another's pains; and, in contradistinction to the Wittgensteinians, we traditionists cannot use publicly observable phenomena, such as another's bodily state, as direct evidence regarding his experiential data. Since knowledge of such a correlation is impossible, we are freed from any duty to provide it. Being impossible, it is of no use and hence of no interest to us. On the other hand, each of us is in possession of a corresponding empirical correlation in his own case, and it is this that we utilize in the analogy argument."

W: "Of course, I wish to make just the objection that you anticipate. The correlation that you need in order to have inductive evidence for the pain of another is a correlation between bodily states and *his* pains. And this, as you confess, is just what you cannot have. At best you possess knowledge of a correlation between bodily states and *your* pains. But this will not help you to know of the pains of another. Having admitted that it is impossible for you to have what the analogy argument requires, you pretend that since it is impossible it is not required. Such reasoning is no more cogent than if one were to say that since to construct a square circle would require the building of a figure that is both curved and rectilinear, which is impossible, then the latter is not really required by the former. You ought, instead, to admit that a traditionist could not possibly use the analogy argument to accomplish his purposes."

T: "I wouldn't argue so foolishly. Were I to admit to

all that you attribute to me, I would indeed have out-raged logic. My position, however, is this: I admit, as you correctly noted, that I cannot employ as my inductive base for inference to another's pain an empirical cor-relation between bodily states and *his* pains. But I deny your assumption that such a correlation is requisite to the legitimate use of the analogy argument. I refuse to grieve over the logical impossibility of my having direct evidence for the mind of another. To do so would be pointless, and it was to this fact that I had reference when I said that the correlation that requires it is neither of use nor of interest to the traditionist. Of course, if, *per impossibile,* we were to possess knowledge of such a correlation, our analogy argument would be as strong as such arguments can be. Indeed, in this case, we would not have need of the analogy argument as our fundamental technique for substantiating propositions regarding other minds: we could use direct evidence freely. But since this *is* impossible, we must content our-selves with the best that is possible. And the best pos-sible, for each of us, consists in the use of an analogy argument that depends upon a correlation between bodily states and *my* pains. This is as close as we can possibly come to the ideal of a complete similarity be-tween the entities that we infer and their analogues on the basis of which we infer. In the present case, the simi-larity is marred by the logically necessary difference be-tween the pain(s) that I infer, namely, *his* pains, and the pains on which I base my inference, namely, *my* pains: it is logically necessary that the pains (of mine) from which I argue be my pains and not his pains, and it is logically necessary that the pains (of his) to which I argue be his pains and not mine. Granted this ineluctable dissimilarity, still the similarities that do obtain are not only the most we could have but are also enough for our purposes. These are the similarities between my pains and the pains that I infer to be his.

"Thus, I defend my rejection of the indirect-evidence principle by repudiating your argument on its behalf. You had contended that one could not inductively establish the existence of an A unless one could establish the existence of a correlation between A's and B's, and that the latter would require the possibility of direct evidence for the existence of A's. In the case before us, A's are *his* pains and B's are *his* bodily states. I admit the impossibility of direct evidence for the existence of A's, but I deny that one must establish a correlation between A's and B's in order to provide inductive evidence for the existence of an A. (I am, of course, willing to grant that one can establish a correlation between A's and B's by means of the analogy argument.) I maintain that a correlation between AT's and BT's will do, instead, where AT's are *my* pains and BT's *my* bodily states, coupled, of course, with the analogy holding between B's and BT's. Notwithstanding the necessary difference between A's and AT's, in that A's are *his* and AT's are *mine*, the similarity between A's and AT's, between *my* pains and the inferred pains (together with the similarity between B's and BT's), will entitle me to infer the existence of A's. Thus, the analogy argument can provide me with indirect evidence for the existence of an A (for *his* being in pain)."

W: "You would have me believe that the only difficulty that besets your analogy argument consists in its weakness compared with others. For example, although we can infer on the basis of a correlation between fires of a certain kind and ashes of a certain kind the existence of more ashes of exactly the same kind, when we employ your analogy argument, we cannot infer on the basis of

a correlation between bodily states of a certain kind and
pains of a certain kind the existence of another pain of
exactly the same kind. For the pain that we infer is the
pain of another person, while the pains in the correlation
are the pains of the arguer. This difference, you would
apparently allow, weakens the argument (by comparison
with the fire-ashes argument); but you wish to say that
this is its only flaw: by and large, you hold, the argument is fine; it is just that it is not so strong as some
other arguments. Indeed, you would discount even this
apparent concession of weakness by saying that since the
dissimilarity between the supposed analogues is a logically necessary dissimilarity, the argument is as good as
it possibly could be. I hope to show you, however, that
such an argument is no good at all: it is not just that,
inevitably, it limps a little, but rather that it is hope-
lessly inoperative.

"To begin, you think that the analogy argument will
provide you with indirect evidence regarding the experiential data of another person. However, the indirect
evidence provided by an inductive analogy argument is
but a surrogate for direct evidence. If the latter is not
so much as possible, the former is without a role to play.
'Indirect' has sense only by way of contrast with 'direct.'
This contrast you have removed: for you admit that you
cannot possibly have direct evidence regarding the mind
of another. You ought then, also, to admit that your
so-called evidence regarding other minds not only is not
direct but also is not inductive or indirect, indeed, is
not evidence at all. You have emptied of all meaning
the expression, 'indirect evidence regarding the mind of
another.' "

T: "While you are right when you indicate that the
meaning of 'indirect evidence regarding the experiential

data of another person' does not, for the traditionist, involve the possibility of direct evidence on the matter, it does not follow that it involves no contrast between the notions of direct and indirect evidence. X is direct evidence for p when X is evidence for p in virtue of the meaning of p. When we traditionists say that bodily states are only indirect evidence for statements regarding other minds, we are saying that their evidential status is a matter, not of definition, but of empirical fact. (Groaning and wincing are evidence that another is in pain only because I have found in my own case that I groan and wince when I am in pain. Had I usually smiled instead, then smiling, not groaning or wincing, would be my indirect evidence for the pain of another.) This is surely important. We might, instead, like you Wittgensteinians, have spoken a language (have used a conceptual scheme) in which certain bodily states are, by definition, evidence regarding another person's experiential data. Thus, the logical impossibility of direct evidence on such matters for a traditionist provides a contrast between the traditionist language (PL_1) and other possible languages, such as that which you employ. Similarly, it provides a contrast between a traditionist's statements about other minds and his statements about physical affairs: for the latter permit of both direct and indirect evidence in contrast with the former.

"I admit that indirect evidence regarding other minds is not a surrogate for direct evidence, but it does not follow from this that it is not evidence at all, nor that it is not inductive or indirect. Of course, an inductive argument from some smoke to a fire is very different from the analogy argument from a bodily state to another's pain: only in the case of the former argument is direct evidence so much as possible. Nevertheless, I refer to both such arguments as inductive arguments.

If you wish, you may emphasize the difference between them by reserving the term 'inductive argument' for arguments of the first kind. Also, if you wish, you may reserve the term 'indirect evidence' for evidence provided by arguments of the first kind. But then we shall only need some new terms for arguments of the second kind and the evidence with which they provide us. For the evidence with which they supply us obviously does not fit the definition of 'direct evidence.' What you may not reasonably do is deny that arguments of the second kind, traditionist analogy arguments regarding other minds, do provide evidence regarding the experiential data of others. Or, rather, you may say this, but your saying so will be tantamount to a refusal to speak a PL_1. You will not, thereby, have proven the unserviceability of a PL_1. You will merely have demonstrated your aversion to this conceptual scheme."

W: "Notice, however, that the contrast that you would afford the notions of direct and indirect evidence, in the case of other minds, is such that you could never have knowledge of the mental state of another. It follows that you could not meaningfully talk of the mind of another. As Wittgenstein says:

> The essential thing about private experience is really not that each person possesses his own exemplar, but that nobody knows whether other people also have *this* or something else. The assumption would thus be possible—though unverifiable—that one section of mankind had one sensation of red and another section another. (*Inv.*, 272)

T: "I do not see that this follows at all. Admittedly, direct evidence regarding the mind of another is impossible for a traditionist. So if this were requisite to knowledge of other minds, such knowledge would be impossible. But it is not requisite. It is enough that we should be able to obtain the kind of indirect evidence that the analogy argument provides. You might object that such evidence at best confers a high probability upon a statement about another's mind, and that this is insufficient for knowledge. But surely this won't do. We all know the truth of many empirical generalizations of the form 'All A's are B's,' and we shall never 'verify' these or 'know' them in any sense that requires that their truth be put beyond the possibility of confutation."

W: "That is not my objection: we Wittgensteinians find no contradiction in the notions of 'probabilistic knowledge' or 'corrigible knowledge.' Rather, my objection is that a traditionist could not even have probabilistic, corrigible knowledge of the mind of another. At best he could say, in any given case, 'That body is in a state like that of mine when I have experiential data of kind ψ; so it seems to me (I am inclined to think) that another person owns that body and has a ψ.' Honesty and accuracy would require him to admit, in any given case, that for all he knows he may be mistaken in attributing a mental state to another. Since in no case can a traditionist know the mind of another, in no case can he speak meaningfully of the mind of another: he cannot even say, 'Probably (or I am inclined to think) that person is in pain.'"

T: "I do not see that you have produced any good reason to think that a traditionist cannot know the mind of another. He may always wish to admit what everyone ought always to admit, that in any given case it is logically possible that one who claims knowledge regarding another's mind be mistaken in his claim. But you've shown no reason why we traditionists cannot, in one or another particular situation, be entitled to claim knowledge regarding another person's mental state. Although it is logically possible that I be wrong in making such a claim, I often have very good evidence, in virtue of the analogy argument, for believing that I am not wrong. Thus, I often have the right to claim knowledge on such matters. What more than this is it reasonable to claim?

"Of course, one might wish an incorrigible certainty. And this wish might lead one to speak in the terms of a Wittgensteinian language (or conceptual scheme) rather than those of a PL_1. Thus, for example, Malcolm has maintained that the existence of certain bodily states puts beyond question the nature of another's experiences.[20] Yet you have just allowed that it is not an objection to the idea of probabilistic or corrigible knowledge that leads you to claim that we traditionists can never know the mind of another. Why then do you continue to insist that we cannot possibly have such knowledge?"

W: "I say that you cannot have such knowledge because nothing can confer probability upon a traditionist's putative claims concerning the experiential data of other persons. There *seem* to be two possibilities with regard to the conclusion of your analogy argument, for example, (p) 'He is in pain': that p is true or that p is false. But, if so, then both of these would remain mere possibilities no matter how much data about your own pains you might accumulate and present in the premises of your argument. You undoubtedly think that you may allow this with impunity, maintaining that while both are possible, even given the data of the premises, never-

[20] "Wittgenstein's *Philosophical Investigations*," *op. cit.*, pp. 112–17, esp. p. 113.

theless the truth of p is rendered probable by the premises. You fail to see, however, that the following two supposed hypotheses are equiprobable with respect to the premises:

(a) Although I have always been in pain when I have had bodily state Ø, no one else is ever in pain when another body is in state Ø.

(b) I have always been in pain when I have had bodily state Ø, and other persons are in pain when other bodies (that are their bodies) are in state Ø.

They are equiprobable with respect to the premises because the premises just do not bear upon the pains of other persons. What has held true of you may or may not hold for other persons or other bodies, and your argument provides *no* basis for a choice between these alternatives. Indeed, contrary to what seems to be the case, these are not alternatives: nor are (a) and (b) hypotheses; nor are the aforementioned 'two possibilities' possibilities. For none of them is so much as meaningful in the mouth of a traditionist. This is because (with respect to the latter clause of each) they are unconnected with any possible experience of a traditionist's: in Wittgenstein's terms, they at best refer to a beetle in a box, and so do not refer at all. As Wittgenstein says:

> If I say of myself that it is only from my own case that I know what the word 'pain' means—must I not say the same of other people too? And how can I generalize the one case so irresponsibly?
> Now someone tells me that *he* knows what pain is only from his own case!—Suppose everyone had a box with something in it: we call it a 'beetle.' No one can look into anyone else's box, and everyone says he knows what a beetle is only by looking at *his* beetle.—Here it would be quite possible for everyone to have some-

thing different in his box. One might even imagine such a thing constantly changing.—But suppose the word 'beetle' had a use in these people's language?— If so it would not be used as the name of a thing. The thing in the box has no place in the language game at all; not even as a *something:* for the box might even be empty.—No, one can 'divide through' by the thing in the box; it cancels out, whatever it is.[21]

Since the supposed inference could never be tested by any means except further inferences of the same kind, it could never be tested at all. An inductive argument by analogy is legitimate only if its legitimacy permits of an independent test. Since the indirect evidence with which your analogy argument allegedly provides you could be compared only with more of the same, it cannot even be indirect evidence. This point finds expression in the indirect-evidence principle, namely: if it is impossible to have direct evidence for p (where p affirms the existence of a particular state of affairs), then it is impossible to have indirect evidence for p. Thus, it is impossible for a traditionist to possess indirect evidence for the conclusion of his analogy argument, that is, for his statement(s) about other minds. And since neither direct nor indirect evidence is possible regarding such alleged statements, the traditionist must grant, in accordance with the testability principle, that they are meaningless."

T: "You argue now in the manner of your earlier arguments (in Ch. II) against the legitimacy of nonindependent checks upon one's memory impressions. Just as you then maintained that one's memory impressions will entitle one to accept the truth of a proposition only if some independent check upon them is possible, so you hold, on the matter at hand, that the analogy argument is legitimate only if some independent check upon its legitimacy is possible. And just as I there replied that I so use my language that the possibility of independent checks is not requisite to the justification-role of memory impressions, so here I reply that my language is such that the legitimacy of the analogy argument does not require the possibility of an independent check upon its legitimacy. Admittedly, the indirect evidence with which the analogy argument provides me is not a surrogate for direct evidence, but it is nonetheless evidence for all that."

W: "But you ought, then, to admit that your so-called language is not even a language, at least when it comes to talking of the experiential data of other persons. For in this case, terms such as 'legitimate analogy argument' and 'indirect evidence' have lost their meaning. Since you cannot possibly have direct evidence regarding the mind of another, indirect evidence and the analogy argument are left with no role to play in this matter. The supposed entities, of whose existence they are called upon to inform us, are but ineffable beetles in boxes. The 'thing in the box . . . cancels out.' You cannot sensibly speak of 'it.' The alleged language (PL_1) in which you profess to speak of other minds turns out to be no language at all. 'We as it were turned a knob which looked as if it could be used to turn on some part of the machine; but it was a mere ornament, not connected with the mechanism at all.' " [22]

T: "I grant you that the experiential data of other persons are beetles in boxes: no one can have direct evidence for the existence of another's beetle: no one

[22] *Inv.*, 270. Cf. Ch. II, Sec. 2.

can feel another's pain. But I would not, on that account, consign them to the realm of the ineffable. It is a fundamental conceptual truth of my traditionist language, my PL_1, that the analogy argument provides evidence for statements about other minds. Thus, indirect evidence is obtainable regarding such statements. Hence, the testability principle is satisfied, and I may speak meaningfully of these beetles, these other minds.

"Nor ought you to find all of this surprising. Every language must have its basic operating principles, that is, fundamental conceptual truths of that language that embody the basic structure of the language. And it would make no sense to demand evidence or justification for these principles. For they are the very principles by reference to which the meaningfulness of, and/or support for, any utterance of the language is to be determined. That first principles are insusceptible of support is as sure as the fallaciousness of circular argument. That such principles are the legitimate and necessary features of language may be seen by noting that the testability principle and the principles of deduction and induction, as well as those principles which reveal the justification-roles of perception and memory, are, at most, formalizations or codifications of the statement-making language-game that all of us 'play.'

"Of course, we (logically) cannot justify the trust we place in deduction, induction, perception, memory, or the testability principle. In ordinary language, it is conceptually true, for example, that one is not making an empirical statement if evidence for or against the truth of his utterance is impossible, and that an empirically discovered correlation between A's and B's provides evidence for 'All A's are B's.' Any skeptic who refuses to recognize the truth of these principles on grounds that we cannot justify them, simply shows that he does not wish to speak ordinary language. Similarly, you point out that I, as a traditionist, cannot independently test the legitimacy of the analogy argument regarding other minds, and you maintain that this argument is therefore illegitimate. Thus, you endeavor to undermine what is for me a basic mode of evidence on the ground that I cannot justify my acceptance of this mode of evidence. In so doing, you merely display the fact that you wish to speak a different kind of language. There is nothing the matter with your manifesting such a wish. But do not think that you have done anything more: in particular, you have not established the unserviceability of a PL_1. You only reveal your aversion to such a language when you refuse to accept its basic operating principles.

"It seems to me that you are being arbitrary when you embrace the indirect-evidence principle. But, then, I am sure that you view as utterly capricious my acceptance of the analogy argument as a basic mode of evidence regarding other minds. I find you unduly intolerant when you preclude as impossible or unintelligible my analogical inferences to the experiential data of others. Yet it is clear that you think me quite illogical when I wish to admit into my language-game entities, namely, other minds, which have the status of beetles in boxes. Thus, it is hard to see how we are to resolve our differences."

W: "Once again (cf. Ch. II) it begins to look as if our disagreement may not be susceptible of settlement. Still, there are further arguments that I wish to level against you."

4) Summary and Prospectus

At this point, we shall interrupt our imaginary dialogue between the Wittgensteinian and the traditionist in order to summarize its results and to look ahead to its future course.

In our opinion, the traditionist has succeeded in defeating the contradiction argument (Sec. 2) and in blunting the effect of the arguments that utilized the direct-evidence principle (Sec. 3b) and the indirect-evidence principle (Sec. 3c).[23] It is the latter arguments that are the most subtle features, yet to be considered, of the Wittgensteinian external attack upon the private object, and it is these to which we have devoted most of this chapter. When we say that the traditionist has blunted the effect of these arguments, we mean that these arguments fall short of being knock-down, sure-fire proofs that a PL_1 is unserviceable. They are not geared to show merely that the private object, *in fact,* plays no role in the logic of *ordinary* language. Indeed, this question, per se, we shall never examine explicitly (cf. Ch. I, Sec. 4). These arguments are calculated to show that the private object *could* play no role in *any* intersubjective language, that a PL_1 is necessarily a PL_2, that is, that a PL_1 is unserviceable. And this they fail to establish

[23] These principles have also been attacked in a way somewhat different from that of our traditionist: cf. C. S. Chihara and J. A. Fodor, "Operationalism and Ordinary Language: A Critique of Wittgenstein," *American Philosophical Quarterly,* II (Oct., 1965); H. Putnam, "Brains and Behavior," in R. J. Butler, ed., *Philosophy,* Second Series (Oxford: Basil Blackwell, 1965).

beyond dispute because the traditionist is willing to utilize the analogy argument as a basic evidence-providing technique with respect to other minds. By means of this tactic, the traditionist hopes to place the Wittgensteinian in the position of refusing to speak a PL_1: that is, the arguments with which the Wittgensteinian would demonstrate the unserviceability of a PL_1 may be transmuted, according to the traditionist, into an insistence upon speaking only those languages (accepting only those conceptual schemes) that allow the possibility of direct evidence for statements about other minds.

Once again, (cf. Ch. II) then, the two parties to our discussion have reached a point of fundamental disagreement over basic principles. The Wittgensteinian affirms, and the traditionist denies, both (a) that an inductive argument by analogy is legitimate only if its legitimacy permits of an independent test, and (b) the indirect-evidence principle. They agree that a traditionist cannot have direct evidence regarding the experiential data of other persons, but they cannot agree upon the significance of this fact. In particular, the traditionist affirms, and the Wittgensteinian denies, the legitimacy of the traditionist's analogy argument and the indirect evidence with which, according to the traditionist, it supplies him. This leads us, once more (cf. Ch. II), to suggest that their differences may comprise not so much a matter of logical fact as a matter of linguistic or logical preference or decision: that it may be a change in attitude rather than fresh points of logic that is requisite to any resolution of this controversy.

In the next chapter, we turn our attention to further Wittgensteinian attacks upon the private object (cf. Ch. I, Sec. 4). These assaults involve an interesting blend of the first and second prongs of the internal attack. Thus, the external attack (the second prong of the internal attack) will not have been abandoned. The coming assaults upon PL_1 consist of arguments to this effect: if a PL_1 could achieve serviceability only in virtue of the traditionist's adoption of the analogy-argument principle, then it would not be serviceable at all, and hence, too, it would be impossible. Since the attacks combine an assault upon the analogy argument—the acceptance of which lies at the root of the traditionist's defense of the serviceability of the private object—with an assault upon the thesis that a PL_1 is possible, they serve, at once, as vehicles of both the external attack upon the private object and also the other prong of the internal attack—the endeavor to establish the impossibility of the private object in light of its unserviceability.

IV |

The Internal Attack: Prongs One and Two

1) Prologue

We come now to the most powerful of all the assaults upon the private object. It is an argument, or series of arguments, developed by P. F. Strawson,[1] which we shall refer to as the *ascription argument*. Just as each of the Wittgensteinian arguments of the preceding chapter may be viewed as an interpretation of *Inv.*, 302, so, too, the ascription argument may be seen as the elaboration of

[1] Cf. P. F. Strawson, *Individuals: An Essay in Descriptive Metaphysics* (London: Methuen and Co. Ltd., 1959), Pt. I, esp., Ch. 3. As has been shown by G. Bird in *Kant's Theory of Knowledge: An Outline of One Central Argument in the "Critique of Pure Reason"* (New York: Humanities Press, 1962), there are significant similarities between Strawson's and Kant's ideas about *persons* and their *experiences*. These similarities make manifest the fact that the antitraditionist line of argument in this chapter has its historical antecedents and is not the exclusive property of any one philosopher.

the central idea of that passage: "If one has to imagine someone else's pain on the model of one's own, this is none too easy a thing to do; for I have to imagine pain that I *do not feel* on the model of the pain that I *do feel*." Whereas the former arguments are devoted to establishing the contradictory or meaningless nature of the conclusion of the analogy argument, the latter is used to show that ". . . not even the syntax of the premises of the inference exists." [2] The former would prove that the analogy argument could not finish, the latter that it could not begin.

The beginning, as we well know, is supposed to consist of premises that affirm the existence of an empirical correlation between one's experiences and one's bodily states. The traditionist would argue, for example: Time and again I have been in pain when in a certain bodily state; that (other) body is in a similar state; hence, there is probably another person, the owner of that body, who is also in pain (cf. Ch. III, Sec. 3b). Thus, the analogy argument would rest the conclusion "He is in pain" upon premises involving the notion "I am in pain." The Wittgensteinian, here drawing upon Strawson's ideas, contends, however, that this conclusion cannot rest upon such premises: for they only *appear* to involve the notion "I am in pain" (cf. *Inv.*, 269). In fact, it is argued, no such notion is available to the traditionist. And, in this case, not only does the analogy argument fail, but also, since the traditionist cannot even entertain an idea such as "I am in pain," a PL_1 is seen to be impossible. We shall now proceed to develop this ascription argument in our own words, not worrying whether our version of the argument exactly matches the text of Strawson's remarks. The subsequent portions of this chapter

[2] Strawson, *op. cit.*, p. 109.

will be devoted to issues generated by the ascription argument.

2) *The Ascription Argument*

The argument may be divided in two, the first argument (i) concluding that the traditionist's language, a PL_1, is unserviceable, and the second argument (ii) concluding that it is, therefore, impossible. Thus, the ascription argument combines within itself both prongs of the internal assault upon the private object. It is for this reason that the present chapter is entitled "The Internal Attack: Prongs One and Two." The argument runs as follows.

(i) The traditionist grants that his only means of obtaining evidence for statements about the experiences of others is the analogy argument. He also accepts the testability principle, in accordance with which one can talk of (make statements about) other minds only if it is possible for one to obtain evidence regarding such statements. Therefore, if it can be shown that the analogy argument will not enable the traditionist to obtain evidence for statements about the experiences of others, it will have been proven that he cannot talk of other minds, that is, that a PL_1 is unserviceable.

The next step is to show that the analogy argument will not enable the traditionist to obtain evidence for statements about the experiences of others. An analogy argument that would provide the traditionist with such evidence would contain premises that ascribe experiences to the traditionist himself, that is, premises that include the notion of *my* experiences. But to employ this notion,

that is, to ascribe experiences to *myself,* one must possess
the notion of *his* experiences; one must be able to ascribe
experiences to others. One is able to talk of the experiences of others only if one is able to obtain evidence
regarding these experiences. The traditionist may claim
that he is able to do this, and he may appeal to some
second analogy argument on behalf of this claim. But
the problem that arose in the case of the initial analogy
argument arises also in the case of the second. To appeal
to some third analogy argument, etc., is merely to commence an infinite regress and is fruitless. Thus, to employ the analogy argument, one must be able to obtain
evidence for statements about the experiences of others
by means other than the analogy argument. Yet it is
admitted on all sides that no other means of obtaining
such evidence is available to the traditionist. It follows
that the analogy argument will not enable the traditionist to obtain evidence for statements about the experiences of others. Therefore, the traditionist cannot
talk of other minds: A PL_1 is unserviceable.

(ii) In accordance with the conclusion of (i), the traditionist cannot make statements about the experiences
of others. But, to repeat a crucial premise of (i), to employ the notion of *my* experiences, that is, to ascribe
experiences to *myself,* one must possess the notion of
his experiences; one must be able to ascribe experiences
to others. It follows that the traditionist has no notion
of *my* experiences; he is unable to ascribe experiences
to *myself.* If any traditionist language, any PL_1, is possible, then the traditionist must possess the notion of
my experiences; he must be able to ascribe experiences
to *myself.* Since it has been shown that he is lacking in
this respect, the traditionist's language, a PL_1, is seen
to be impossible. In short, the traditionist cannot treat
the notions of *I* and *my experiences* as logically primi-

tive with respect to the notions of *he* and *his experiences,* because one who does not possess the latter notions is lacking the former notions as well.

3) The Ascription Principle

Both of the arguments, (i) and (ii), which compose the ascription argument, hinge upon the premise that we shall call the *ascription principle:* To employ the notion of *my* experiences, that is, to ascribe experiences to *myself,* one must have the notion of *his* experiences, that is, one must be able to ascribe experiences to others. It is therefore imperative that we inquire into the credentials of this principle:

> The main point here is a purely logical one: the idea of a predicate is correlative with that of a *range* of distinguishable individuals of which the predicate can be significantly, though not necessarily truly, affirmed.[3]

It is senseless to suppose that one might lack the notion of *he* (*you, they,* etc.) and nevertheless possess the notion of *I.* If one has the notion of any particular self, say *myself,* then one must have the notion of *self* and, consequently, must be able to distinguish other selves. Similarly, it is senseless to suppose that one might lack the notion of his experiences and, nevertheless, possess the notion of *my experiences.* If one possesses the notion of any particular person's having an experience, say *my experience,* then one must possess the notion of *having an experience* and, consequently, must be able to dis-

[3] Strawson, *op. cit.,* p. 99, n. 1.

tinguish other persons who have experiences. If some-
body were forced to confess "I could never tell whether
there are any selves other than myself" or "I could never
tell whether experiences are had by any persons other
than me," it could be concluded that he had no notion
either of self or of having an experience.

4) The Traditionist's Attempt to Cope with the Ascription Argument

It seems to us that, for the first time in this book, the
traditionist is forced really to give ground: the power
of the ascription argument is not without effect upon any
perspicacious defender of the private object. Let us re-
turn to dialogue form and see how such a traditionist
might endeavor to meet this new argument.

4a) THE TRADITIONIST MODIFIES HIS POSITION

T: "Strawson has, indeed, taught us something by
means of his ascription argument. We traditionists have
usually taken an *egocentric* approach to the epistemological problem of how we may justify our beliefs about
the world. We have viewed the problem as the *egocentric
predicament,* whereby one must begin 'at home' with his
own experiential data (his own private objects) and must
somehow attempt to 'go abroad' (cf. Ch. I, Sec. 3–3d).
Strawson would tell us, however, not only that we cannot 'go abroad,' but, worse, that we have not even so
much as 'a home': according to the ascription argument,

we do not even possess a notion of ourselves and our own experiential data.

"I do not see that we can deal adequately with the ascription argument by repudiating the ascription principle. Whereas classical traditionists such as Descartes, Locke, Berkeley, and Hume, as well as contemporary traditionists such as Russell, Lewis, Broad, Price, and Ayer, have often thought it unproblematic to commence their philosophizing upon the base of the 'hard data' consisting of '*my* experiential data,' Strawson has taught us that this is an incoherent point of departure. So long as my right to say anything at all about the minds of others is in question, I have no right to assume that I may speak meaningfully of my own mind. (Thus, too, it seems clear that solipsism is an untenable, because incoherent, position [cf. Ch. I, Sec. 3d].)

"I do not believe, however, that the ascription argument destroys the private object, that is, the idea of a PL_1. In particular, I think that the traditionist ought now to take a somewhat different approach. Although the traditionist cannot employ the analogy argument in order to *infer* 'his experiences' on the logically prior basis of 'my experiences,' he may nevertheless use the technique of this argument as a device for *constructing* 'my experiences' and 'his experiences,' that is, the language of 'I' and 'he,' out of *pure* (i.e., unowned) experiential data. I would suggest that this may be done as follows.

"One may take note of correlations between experiences of certain kinds and bodily states of certain kinds of a particular body, say body X. For example, suppose that pains have been regularly correlated with Ø-states of X. One may also have noted both that other bodies are sometimes Ø, and that pains are correlated only with Ø-states of X, not with the Ø-states of other bodies. For some time, one has spoken (or thought) only of experiences as such and of bodies as such, never of my (or his) pain or my (or his) body. But now at one stroke, as it were, one introduces together the notions of both *I* and *he*: that is, one begins to speak or think of the experiences one has as 'my experiences,' and one begins to ascribe experiences to other persons on the basis of correlations between experiences and states of X. For example, when one has a pain one says (or thinks) 'I am in pain,' and when one has noted a correlation between pains and X's Ø-states, and body Y is also Ø, one says 'He is in pain.' "

W: "Are you doing psychology? Are you claiming that this is how each of us has come by our conceptual equipment as it pertains to persons?"

T: "No. That is an empirical matter for psychologists and other scientists to decide. I contend only that the situation that I have described is logically possible, and this is enough for my purposes. My aim here is to repudiate the ascription argument in so far as it is geared to show the impossibility or the unserviceability of a PL_1 per se. I grant that the ascription argument establishes both the unserviceability and, indeed, the impossibility of any would-be PL_1 that would begin with, or treat as primitive, the concepts of *I* and of *my experiences*. In light of the ascription principle, I must confess that one could neither employ such a language as a base for the derivation of a language in which one speaks of the experiences of others, nor even speak such a language. Such a PL_1 would be neither serviceable nor possible, and this is no small concession. It is no minor achievement on the part of Strawson to have shown that traditionists have been misguided in this, their usual approach to epistemology. Nevertheless, I wish to maintain that a PL_1 is both possible and serviceable. It is to this end that I have put forward my hypothetical situation. I now maintain that a language whose notions of *I* and *he* are derivative with respect to a PL_1 of pure, or unowned, experiences is itself a PL_1 that is both possible and serviceable. The pure-experience PL_1 upon which it is based is unserviceable in the sense that two persons, each of whom speak such a PL_1 but neither of whom can speak person language, could not talk to each other about their experiences. Nevertheless, it is my position that it is serviceable in the sense that it may be understood by those who speak a language whose notions of *I* and *he* are derived from it, and also in the sense that it is logically primitive with respect to a language of the latter sort.

"I am aware that you Wittgensteinians view ordinary language as a language in which the concepts of *his experiences* and *my experiences* are logically dependent upon publicly observable phenomena. We traditionists deny this. Yet the struggle between us does not (in this book) take the form of a debate as to which of our positions, in fact, provides the more accurate characterization of ordinary language. This question we deal with only to the extent that it is involved in the issue to which we do here devote ourselves: is it or is it not the case that a PL_1 is possible and serviceable? (cf. Ch. I, Sec. 4; Ch. III, Sec. 4). Thus, if I can show that a language in which experiences are ascribed to persons may be viewed as a PL_1 that is logically derivative with respect to a PL_1 in which one speaks of pure or unowned experiences, then I shall have won the debate in which we are engaged. If, on the other hand, victory is to be yours, you must demonstrate the unserviceability, indeed the impossibility, of a PL_1."

W: "It seems clear, at least, that a great deal of proving and defending lies before you. I hope that your plans and your position will also become clear as we proceed. For a starter, I should like you to explain how it can possibly be that a language of persons (*person language*) may be viewed as 'logically derivative with respect to a PL_1 in which one speaks of pure or unowned experiences.' In particular, I wish to know how someone, S, who lacks the notion of a person, can possibly speak of *unowned* experiences. If he can talk about pure experiences, musn't he also be able to talk about *im*pure experiences? If S has the concept of unowned experience, mustn't he also have the concept of *owned* experience? Otherwise, what would it mean for S to think of an experience as unowned? But the concept of an owned experience involves the idea of an owner, a person. Hence, it would seem that one who lacks the concept of a person cannot possibly speak of pure or unowned experiences, and the language of pure experiences (*pure-experience language*) could not possibly be logically primitive with respect to person language."

T: "You mistake my meaning. When I say that S speaks of pure or unowned experiences, I mean that he thinks (talks) of experiences neither as having owners nor as lacking owners. As you indicate, lacking the concept of a person, he cannot think (speak) of experiences as belonging or not belonging to a person: for he cannot think of a person. Thus, he thinks of experiences as such, experiences (period). He does not conceive of experiences as being owned or unowned (pure or impure) any more than someone who has no notion of legal property conceives of a tree as being owned or unowned. Thus, when I say that S, who lacks the notion of a person, speaks a pure-experience language, I don't mean that S speaks of persons as not owning experiences (i.e., of experiences as not being owned by persons) but, rather, that although S thinks of experiences, he does not at all think of persons. This being so, the objection you mention does not apply to my position."

W: "Having clarified this much of your position, will you tell me how the language of persons (or person language), which you claim to be constructible from a pure-experience language, can possibly qualify for the title 'PL₁'? You admit that the notion of *I* is indissolubly linked with the notion of *he,* and your hypothetical situation seems to reveal that one is to base one's talk of 'his experiences' (experiences of another person) upon correlations between experiences and bodily states. Doesn't this mean that the experiential terms of person language are logically dependent upon publicly observable phenomena? In this case, the language in question is not a PL₁.

"Prior to your acceptance of the ascription principle it looked as if you were free to employ the analogy argument, basing your talk about others upon correlations between experiences and bodily states without commitment to the idea that a reference to bodily states is part of the meaning of experiential terms. Having accepted this principle, you confess that you cannot utilize the analogy argument in the usual way—as an inductive inference from propositions about *my* experiences to propositions about *his* experiences. You now wish to employ the technique of this argument in the very introduction of the terms 'his experiences' and 'my experiences.' But this is the technique of using correlations between experiences and publicly observable phenomena in order to provide evidence regarding the experiences of other persons. It would seem, then, that the experiential terms

so introduced are not conceptually independent of publicly observable phenomena. Thus, the language in question could hardly be a PL_1."

4b) FURTHER MODIFICATIONS OF THE TRADITIONIST POSITION

T: "Once again you force me to give ground. I should,
of course, like to deny flatly your allegation, for to grant
it at all would seem to imperil my entire position. Nevertheless, candor compels me to allow the merit of your
point. So we must now reexamine, in light of this point,
the traditionist stand that I have just sketched.

"For one thing, your attack, aimed as it is at my person language, leaves unscathed my contention that a PL_1
of pure experiences is possible. Still, I have admitted that
the latter language is, in an important sense, unserviceable: namely, two persons who speak such a language but
who lack the concept of a person could not communicate
about their experiences. Thus, in order to show that a
PL_1 is both possible and serviceable (in the foregoing
sense of 'serviceable'), I should be obliged to establish
this regarding the person language that I have under-
taken to defend. I must therefore take very seriously
your contention that this language cannot be a PL_1.

"I admit that the person language that I have sketched
does not fully satisfy the requirements of a PL_1, and this
is so for just the reasons you mention. There is a conceptual bond between the notions of *my experiences* and
his experiences in that to employ either notion one must
be able to employ the other. Further, it is conceptually
true that it is correlations between experiences and
bodily states that provide one with a basis for one's
statements about the experiences of others (*his* experiences). It follows that the experiential terms of this

language are not conceptually independent of publicly observable phenomena. Thus, too, it follows that this person language does not satisfy the definition of a PL$_1$, that is, is not a PL$_1$."

W: "Having admitted so much, I wonder why you seemed to qualify your admission by saying that the person language does not *fully* satisfy the requirements of a PL$_1$. After all, a PL$_1$ has been defined as 'a language each word of which refers to experiential data, although each of these words is conceptually independent of publicly observable phenomena' (cf. Ch. I, Sec. 2). You allow that the experiential terms of the person language are not conceptually independent of publicly observable phenomena. I therefore see no justification for the reservations implied by the above-mentioned qualification."

T: "You are right. My use of that qualifying phrase was misleading. And I must now plainly say that the person language is *not* a PL$_1$. Nevertheless, I employed the qualifying phrase for good reason, a reason that does not in any way alter the concession I have made, but which, perhaps, reveals that traditionism retains considerable merit despite the concession.

"My point is this. You Wittgensteinians maintain that the logic of experiential terms is such that certain bodily states provide one with *direct* evidence (cf. Ch. III, Sec. 3a) for the ascription of an experience to another person. For example, you would hold that it is a conceptual truth that, in a somewhat specifiable context, the groaning of another is evidence that this other person is in pain. We traditionists, on the other hand, view the connection between bodily states and experiences as contingent, so that the bodily states of another contribute only *indirect* evidence for the ascription of an experience to another person. For example, we would say that it is not a conceptual truth but an empirical matter of fact that, in a somewhat specifiable context, the groaning of another is evidence that this other person is in pain. Had smiling rather than groaning been correlated with the experience of pain, then it would be smiling rather than groaning that would be evidence that another person is in pain. I believe that we traditionists may cling to this view even though we allow that the person language is not a PL_1. This means that even though reference to publicly observable phenomena, namely, bodily states, is essential to the ascription of experiences to persons, no reference to any particular kind of bodily state is essential for ascribing any particular kind of experience to a person. For example, although *some* bodily states must, as a matter of logic, count as evidence for another person's being in pain, whether such states be groaning, smiling, or what have you will be determined not by logic but by the course of experience. The conceptual truth is not that groaning counts as evidence for another person's being in pain but, rather, that the bodily states (*whatever* they are) correlated with pains in one's own experience provide one with evidence for the pains of others.

"For the Wittgensteinian, there is nothing to a person's experience except all of the behavioral indicators that, as a matter of logic, count as evidence for the existence of his experience. There is no nonbehavioral or mentalistic residue when all such behavioral factors are abstracted from the notion of experience. And this, it seems to me, is a distortion of what we all mean to talk about when we ascribe experiences to persons. The merit of traditionism, in contrast, lies in the fact that we traditionists do justice to the nonbehavioral or mentalistic element of experience. We accomplish this by refusing to treat the connection between any particular kind of experience and any particular kind of behavior as a logical or definitional connection. And I think that we may persevere in this course even though we admit that each particular kind of experience that a person undergoes must, as a matter of the logic of person language, be connected with *some* kind of behavior *or other*.

"My revised position, then, comes to this: A pure-experience PL_1 is possible. It is unserviceable in the important sense that two persons who speak such a language but who have no concept of a person cannot communicate about their experiences. But it is serviceable in the sense that a person language may be constructed from it and also in the sense that one who speaks such a person language can understand the talk of one who speaks a pure-experience PL_1. The person language is not a PL_1. Nevertheless, the meanings of its experiential terms do not consist merely in their connections with bodily states: these terms designate the sorts of experiences designated by the terms of a pure-experience PL_1 although they refer to such experiences not as pure or unowned experiences but as the experiences *of* persons. This nonbehavioral content of the experiential terms of the person language is a result of the fact that the person language is constructed from the more primitive pure-experience language."

W: "It is inaccurate of you to characterize the Wittgensteinian position as one according to which 'there is nothing to a person's experience except all of the behavioral indicators that, as a matter of logic, count as evidence for the existence of his experience.' Consider, for example, the following remarks of Malcolm's and Strawson's:

The thought that behind someone's pain-behavior is the pain itself does not enter into our use of 'He's in pain,' but what does enter into it is our sympathetic, or unsympathetic, reaction to him. The fact that the latter does enter into our use of that sentence (but might not have) gives sense to saying that the sentence 'He is in pain' does not just *mean* that his behavior, words, and circumstances are such and such—although these are the criteria for its use.[4]

If one is playing a game of cards, the distinctive markings of a certain card constitute a logically adequate criterion for calling it, say, the Queen of Hearts; but, in calling it this, in the context of the game, one is ascribing to it properties over and above the possession of these markings. The predicate gets its meaning from the whole structure of the game. So with the language in which we ascribe P-predicates [namely, predicates which '. . . imply the possession of consciousness on the part of that to which they are ascribed . . .' [5]]. To say that the criteria on the strength of which we ascribe P-predicates to others are of a logically adequate kind for this ascription, is not to say that all there is to the ascriptive meaning of these predicates is these criteria. To say this is to forget that they are P-predicates, to forget the rest of the language-structure to which they belong.[6]

Still, it is not to our purpose here to worry about the important intricacies of the views inherent in the quoted remarks. Having said only this much, by way of setting the record straight regarding the Wittgensteinian position, I shall nevertheless accept something close to what

[4] N. Malcolm, "Wittgenstein's *Philosophical Investigations*," *Knowledge and Certainty: Essays and Lectures* (Englewood Cliffs, N.J.: Prentice-Hall, Inc., 1963), pp. 118–19; cf. pp. 117–20. In *Inv.*, 287, Wittgenstein remarks: "Pity, one may say, is a form of conviction that someone else is in pain." Cf. *Inv.*, 284, 286.
[5] Strawson, *op. cit.*, p. 105.
[6] *Ibid.*, p. 110.

you said in describing our position: there is no nonbehavioral or mentalistic residue when *all* behavioral factors are abstracted from the notion of experience. Let
us now see exactly what differences remain to divide
traditionism from Wittgensteinianism.

"You have traveled far from your initial stand on the
matters before us, and these differences, consequently,
have decreased. You no longer maintain that a person
language is a PL_1. You have thus abandoned that classical traditionism that holds that one's knowledge of the
world begins 'at home' with *my* experiential data. You
nevertheless cling to a version of traditionism according
to which one's knowledge of the world begins, in another
sense, 'at home': you now hold, that is, that at the logical foundation of such knowledge lies a realm of pure
(unowned) experiential data, and that a person language
can be constructed from the PL_1 in which one speaks
(or thinks) of such data. Thus, you maintain that the
logic of the person language, in which persons may communicate about their experiences, is such as to contain
a reference to the very experiential data that may be
referred to in a pure-experience PL_1. We Wittgensteinians, on the other hand, deny the possibility of such a
pure-experience PL_1, and, consequently, deny the possibility of such a person language as that to which you
subscribe. Instead, we insist that experiences may be
referred to only in a language the significance of whose
experiential terms resides exclusively in their connections
with publicly observable phenomena. We deny the possibility of the private object, and hence we deny the
possibility both of a pure-experience PL_1 and also of a
person language, even *part* of the significance of whose
experiential terms consists in their connection with private objects."

T: "This seems a fair statement of the differences between us. I have briefly indicated how, in my view, one might construct the person language from a pure-experience language. I am anxious to hear your objections."

W: "I should like you further to clarify what you meant when you said (in Sec. 4a): 'Although the traditionist cannot employ the analogy argument in order to *infer* "his experiences" on the logically prior basis of "my experiences," he may nevertheless use the technique of this argument as a device for *constructing* "my experiences" and "his experiences," that is, the language of "I" and "he," out of *pure* (i.e., unowned) experiential data.' Just how is this 'constructing' to be done, and in what sense is the 'technique' of the analogy argument to be utilized?"

4c) THE TRADITIONIST FURTHER CLARIFIES HIS POSITION

T: "Well, for reasons that you yourself have brought to our attention, the analogy argument cannot be viewed as a bridge that enables one to proceed from a logically prior knowledge of *my* experiences to a knowledge of *his* experiences. Nevertheless, one may put the argument to work in the following way. There is (let us suppose) a person, S, who has no concept of himself or any self, but who has a concept both of experiences and of bodies. He can speak or think of experiences (and bodies) as being of various kinds and as being possessed of their properties in varying degrees. He thinks, for example: 'The pain that went on at the time the apple fell from the tree was more severe than the pain that is occurring now, although the former pain lasted longer than the

feeling of warmth that occurred just after the apple
fell.' S has found empirical correlations between experiences of certain kinds and bodily states of certain kinds
of the body X. For example, he has noticed that there
is a certain kind of pain, $\emptyset$, when and only when the
body X is in the state $\emptyset$, and similarly for other experiences and other states of X. S has also found that
experiences are not regularly correlated with the states
of any other bodies. Next, let us suppose, S begins to
speak of persons in the following ways. On those occasions when he would previously have said 'There is now
a $\emptyset$,' he now says 'I have a $\emptyset$.' On those occasions when
he would previously have said 'The body X is trem-
bling,' he now says 'I am trembling.' On those occasions
when he would previously have said 'The body Y is
trembling,' he now says 'He is trembling.' And on both
those occasions when he would previously have said
'There is now a $\emptyset$' and those occasions when he would
previously have said 'There is not now a $\emptyset$,' he now
says 'He has a $\emptyset$,' *provided that* he has found an empirical correlation between $\emptyset$'s and the $\emptyset$-states of X,
and provided also that he finds that the body Y is $\emptyset$.

"When S now says 'He has a $\emptyset$,' S means to talk about
the same kind of experience of which he used to speak
in saying 'There is a $\emptyset$.' And when S says 'I have a $\emptyset$,'
S ascribes to himself the same sort of experience that
he ascribes to another when he says 'He has a $\emptyset$.'
Whereas S used to speak of pure experiences, he now
speaks of the experiences-of-persons. He bases his talk of
my experiences, quite as much as his talk of *his* experiences, upon his knowledge of those pure experiences
that, in the person language, he refers to as 'my experiences.' Thus, S does not treat 'I' as a notion independent of 'he' but introduces, or begins to employ, both
together. Whereas S could not formerly distinguish (or

speak of) two different experiences of exactly the same kind as occurring at the same time, he now may do so by distinguishing, for example, *his* $\emptyset$ from *my* $\emptyset$.

"Thus, a person, S, may 'construct' a language in which experiences are ascribed to persons out of a pure-experience language in the sense that the experiences to which the terms of the latter refer constitute, in part, S's basis for the ascription of experiences to persons. Of course, this basis is not to be identified with S's grounds for the ascription of experiences to himself, as it is for the ascription of experiences to others: for when one undergoes an experience one has every right to ascribe it to oneself, even though one does not do so on the basis of grounds (in the sense of propositions to which one would appeal in support of one's ascription). The 'technique' of the analogy argument is utilized in that it is built into the logic of the person language: it is the analogy between a bodily state of Y and those bodily states of X that have been correlated with experiences of kind $\emptyset$ that, as a matter of logic, justifies S in ascribing to another person an experience of kind $\emptyset$. And, since 'I' and 'he' are logically linked, it is this analogy, too, that makes possible S's ascription of experiences to himself, even though S has no grounds (in the foregoing sense of 'grounds') for ascriptions of the latter sort.

"I would further maintain that this person language is not a PL_2, or, alternatively stated, that it is serviceable: since S can talk about and know about the experiences of another person, W, there is no reason why it should not be possible for S to teach this language to W. S and W can employ the person language in order to exchange information about their experiences. Once they acquire the person language, either of them can come to *understand* the other's pure-experience language, although neither of them can use a pure-experience language to ascribe experiences to himself or to another person. Thus, we may say that no two persons *speak* the same pure-experience language: an intersubjective person language may therefore be viewed as a 'construction' out of not just one pure-experience language but as many pure-experience languages as there are persons who speak such a person language."

5) *Wittgensteinian Criticism*

W: "I find a good deal to object to in your present position. To begin with, your description of S's situation involves both empirical falsehood and logical inconsistency. You say:

> S has found empirical correlations between experiences of certain kinds and bodily states of certain kinds of the body X. For example, he has noticed that there is a certain kind of pain $\emptyset$ when and only when the body X is in the state $\emptyset$, and similarly for other experiences and other states of X. S has also found that such experiences are not regularly correlated with the states of any other bodies.

"You clearly mean to talk of certain ordinary experiences, that, in fact, many different persons undergo. Therefore, you are committed to the (twofold) empirical falsehood: there is a body upon the condition of which all such experiences are (causally or empirically) dependent for their occurrence, and there is no other body upon the condition of which any such experience is dependent for its occurrence.[7] In fact, however, Saunders has

---

[7] Cf. *ibid.*, pp. 90–103, esp. p. 97: "The proposition that *all* experiences are causally dependent on the state of a single

toothaches that are dependent upon the condition of his body but not upon the condition of Henze's body, whereas Henze has toothaches that are not dependent upon the condition of Saunders' body but are dependent upon the condition of his own body.

"The logical inconsistency may be brought out as follows. Once he speaks the person language, S ascribes experiences to others in accordance with the technique of the analogy argument: as you put it, 'he now says "He has a $\emptyset$," *provided that* he has found an empirical correlation between $\emptyset$'s and the $\emptyset$-states of X, and provided also that he finds that the body Y is $\emptyset$.' Presuming that S is usually correct when he thus ascribes experiences to others, it follows that the correlation between $\emptyset$'s and the $\emptyset$-states of X is paralleled by a correlation between $\emptyset$'s and the $\emptyset$-states of Y. Thus, S will have found that such experiences are regularly correlated not only with the states of X but also with the states of other bodies. This is inconsistent with your above-quoted statement: 'S has also found that such experiences are not regularly correlated with the states of any other bodies.'"

T: "It is easy to understand how you might think that these are difficulties for my position. Your reasoning is cogent, and I should indeed be caught in these absurdities if my view were as you here depict it. Therefore, I must further clarify my position and show that I am not committed to these absurdities.

---

body B, for example, is just false . . ." and p. 101, "So long as we persist in talking . . . of experiences on the one hand, and bodies on the other, the most I may be allowed to have noted is that experiences, *all* experiences, stand in special relation to body M, that body M is unique in just this way, that this is what makes body M unique among bodies."

"It must be kept in mind that at one time (t_1) S speaks a pure-experience language, while later (at t_2) he speaks the person language. Suppose that S does not have a Ø at t_1 and that another person, W, does have a Ø at t_1. Suppose that S says at t_1, 'There are no Ø's at t_1,' and S says at t_2, 'There was a Ø at t_1.' The statement made by S at t_1 is a statement in a pure-experience language and is true. The statement made by S at t_2 is a statement in the person language and is true. The two statements do not conflict. Since at t_2, S is speaking the person language, his statement at t_2 is equivalent to 'Someone had a Ø at t_1,' which is true. Since, at t_1, S does not possess the concept of a person's having an experience, his statement at t_1 is not equivalent to the falsehood: 'No one has a Ø at t_1.' His statement at t_1 is true if and only if S does not have a Ø at t_1, and hence it is true. This last sentence reveals the truth conditions of the statement made by S at t_1. S can, *in this way*, state its truth conditions at t_2, but not at t_1, because at t_2, but not at t_1, he has the concept of a person. For the same reason, it would be incorrect to say that S's statement at t_1 is *equivalent* to 'S does not have a Ø at t_1.' Since S does not possess the concept of a person at t_1, S would, at that time, state its truth conditions by saying: 'There are no Ø's at t_1' is true if and only if it is not the case that there is a Ø at t_1.'

"We may now apply these considerations to the criticisms you make. When I described the initial situation of S (at t_1, say) by saying that S has found that certain kinds of experiences occur when and only when a certain body is in certain states and that such experiences are not regularly correlated with the states of any other bodies, I was putting the matter as S, himself, might put it at t_1. I grant you that I meant to talk of certain ordinary experiences, that, in fact, different persons undergo. But since I was speaking from the point of view of S, at t_1, I must be understood as saying only what S himself would say at t_1. Since S does not, at t_1, possess the concept of a person, he can hardly be taken to maintain the falsehoods that all such experiences *of persons* are (empirically or causally) dependent upon the condition of a certain body or that such experiences *of persons* are not regularly correlated with the states of any other bodies. For the same reason, he simply is not talking about any experiences but his own. He is not, of course, talking of his own experiences in the sense that he employs the concepts of 'I' or 'my experience.' But he is talking about them, and only them, in the sense that what he says about experiences is true if and only if certain things hold of his experiences.

"Thus, both the (twofold) empirical falsehood and the logical inconsistency that you attribute to me fail to materialize. Since I was speaking from the point of view of S at t_1, to commit myself to 'There is a body upon the condition of which all such experiences are (causally or empirically) dependent for their occurrence, and there is no other body upon the condition of which any such experience is dependent for its occurrence' was to commit myself to a proposition that is true if and only if there is a body upon the condition of which all such experiences *of S's* are (causally or empirically) dependent for their occurrence, and there is no other body upon the condition of which any such experience *of S's* is dependent for its occurrence. Since the latter is true of S (as we may easily suppose), the proposition to which I committed myself was not the (twofold) empirical falsehood covering persons other than S, to which you alluded, but an empirical truth about the experiences

of S. So, too, I did not commit myself to anything inconsistent with S's discovery, at t_2, that such experiences are
regularly correlated not only with the states of X but
also with the states of other bodies.

"The empirical falsehood and the inconsistency would
materialize only for one who was speaking the person
language: and S, or rather I, from the point of view of
S (at t_1), was speaking not the person language but a
pure-experience language. At t_2, speaking the person language, S can say, as any of us can say in person language,
that such utterances, when made in person language,
involve empirical falsehood and inconsistency. We can
also say, in person language, that the statements made by
S, at t_1, in pure-experience language, do not involve
these errors. For the discourse of S, at that time, is
confined in its application to S's own experiences, even
though S could not tell us this at that time."

W: "You seem to want to have your cake and eat it
too. Let us work with the simple model that you ad-
vance. You say that, at t_1, S truly says. 'There are no $\emptyset$'s
at t_1.' Yet you also say that there was a $\emptyset$ at t_1, namely,
W's $\emptyset$. You think you may escape inconsistency by de-
claring that S was speaking only of his own $\emptyset$'s. This dec-
laration, however, leads you into the further difficulty
that S could not speak of his own $\emptyset$'s at t_1, since he did
not then possess the concept of a person. To dodge this
difficulty, you hold that S's discourse 'is confined in its application to S's own experiences, even though S could not
tell us this at that time.' But by what right can you say
that S's discourse was so confined when, lacking the concept of self, he could not formulate (even to himself) the
idea of its being so confined? It seems clear that S could
put no such restriction upon 'There are no $\emptyset$'s at t_1,'

and, therefore, that he could only have made the false claim that at t_1 there are no $\cancel{V}$'s whatever."

T: "I categorically reject your conclusion. The claim that at t_1 there are no $\cancel{V}$'s whatever is false if and *only if* the speaker's concept of $\cancel{V}$ is the concept of *a person's having a $\cancel{V}$*. If, as in the case of S at t_1, the speaker's concept of $\cancel{V}$ is the concept of *unowned experience*, then the occurrence of W's $\cancel{V}$ is irrelevant to the speaker's claim. The only relevant $\cancel{V}$'s are S's $\cancel{V}$'s, and since S did not have a $\cancel{V}$ at t_1, his claim was true. You seem to think that because S lacked the concept of *self* and hence could not assert that he meant to speak only of his own experiences, he therefore must have meant to speak of the experiences of any person whatever. But that is absurd: since he lacked the concept of *self*, he cannot have *meant* to speak of the experiences *of persons*. Admittedly, then, he did not *mean* to speak of *my* (i.e., S's) experiences. He meant to speak of *pure* (unowned) experiences. It is nonetheless true, as I supposed in sketching the example, that S says (or thinks) 'There is now a $\cancel{V}$,' etc., when he has a $\cancel{V}$ and says (or thinks) 'There is not now a $\cancel{V}$,' etc., when he does not have a $\cancel{V}$. It is in *this* sense that his discourse is confined to his own experiences. Of course S cannot, at t_1, say that he means to talk about his experiences as distinct from the experiences of others: for at t_1 he has no concept of self. But, then, it is absurd for you to make this demand of S as a condition for his possession of a concept of *pure experience*. Yet this is precisely what you do when you claim that his utterance at t_1, 'There are no $\cancel{V}$'s at t_1,' is false because W had a $\cancel{V}$ at t_1. In making the latter claim you beg the question at issue: you simply suppose that a pure-experience language is impossible when you

demand that one who speaks such a language be able
to talk of persons; this is to demand that the pure-
experience be, not a pure-experience language, but a
person language; it is to 'demand it out of existence.' "

W: "Your position is surely clearer than it was. I
now understand that you mean to say: When S speaks
only a pure-experience language, S says 'There is a $\emptyset$ at
t_1' when S has a $\emptyset$ at t_1, and S says 'There is not a $\emptyset$
at t_1' when S does not have a $\emptyset$ at t_1; a statement of
the former sort is true if and only if S has a $\emptyset$ at t_1, and
a statement of the latter sort is true if and only if S
does not have a $\emptyset$ at t_1; and it is the fact that S rather
consistently makes such true statements that constitutes
him a speaker of a pure-experience language. I see, too,
that it will not do for me to beg the question in the way
you mention, by supposing that unless S can say that he
means to confine his remarks to the topic of his own
experiences, his utterance, 'There are no $\emptyset$'s at t_1,' is
false when W has a $\emptyset$ at t_1.

"However, I wish to pursue the general line of my
criticism from a different angle. I have been contending
that when S tries to state, in pure-experience language,
what we would state in person language by saying that
S is not having a $\emptyset$, S is forced, in effect, to deny that
others are having $\emptyset$'s. The point of this criticism is that
S cannot single out his own experiences and say something about them as distinct from the experiences of
others. This, in a sense, you grant, but you maintain that
S may nevertheless talk about those experiences that are,
in fact, his own experiences, even though he cannot refer
to them as experiences *of his*. My point, in general, however, is that one, such as S at t_1, who has no concept of
persons, could not single out experiences in such a way
that he may be said to speak a language in which he

talks about experiences. Let me now attempt to give this point force in the following, and different, way. There appears to be no problem in the idea that S's statement at t_1, 'There is a $\emptyset$ at t_1,' is true when S has a $\emptyset$ at t_1. But I suggest that this appearance is, at least in part, due to the fact that, as speakers of person language, we all know how to be more specific: we need not make such a general statement, and can say instead, 'S has a $\emptyset$ at t_1.' This capacity, however, is not possessed by S when he has no concept of persons and speaks a pure-experience language. Therefore, at t_1, S cannot single out, or identify, a particular experience, a particular $\emptyset$, and say anything about it. In person language, we can identify a particular experience as *the* experience of a certain kind had by a certain person at a given time: it is the reference to a particular person that enables us to single out one particular experience of a certain kind from any other experiences of that kind that might also occur at the time. Since this mode of identifying a particular experience is not open to S, it would seem that he cannot make such identifications.[8] But if he cannot speak identifyingly of a particular experience, he cannot be said to make or understand general statements such as 'There is a $\emptyset$ at t_1.' For such general statements could be made or understood only if one were able to make or understand a statement about a particular $\emptyset$. And this one cannot do if one has no way of singling out, or making an identifying reference to, a particular $\emptyset$."

[8] Cf. *ibid.*, p. 97: ". . . if we think, once more [cf. pp. 40–50], of the requirements of identifying reference in speech to *particular* states of consciousness, or private experiences, we see that such particulars cannot be thus identifyingly referred to except as the states or experiences *of* some identified *person*."

T: "I must remind you that when, in elaborating my position, I contrasted the earlier situation of S (at t_1), in which S speaks a pure-experience language and not a person language, with the later situation of S (at t_2), in which S speaks a person language, I said the following: 'Whereas S could not formerly distinguish (or speak of) two different experiences of exactly the same kind as occurring at the same time, he now may do so by distinguishing, for example, *his ∅* from *my ∅*.' Since, at t_1, S lacks the concept of a person, he is unable to make the foregoing distinction. But it does not follow that he is then unable to single out, or identifyingly refer to, a particular ∅. To do so, he need only specify the time of its occurrence and its exact nature (exactly what kind of a ∅ it is). Far from its following from his inability to distinguish *his ∅* from *my ∅* that he cannot single out a particular ∅, it is just because of this inability that it is a conceptual truth of S's pure-experience language that no two experiences of exactly the same kind occur at the same time. (You may compare this to the logical status of Leibniz's Principle of the Identity of Indiscernibles in that philosopher's system.) It follows that if S had an experience of exactly such-and-such kind at time t, and S now thinks, 'There was an experience of exactly such-and-such kind at time t,' then S may be said to identify (in thought) a particular experience—S is justified in saying (thinking): '*the* experience of exactly such-and-such kind at time t . . .' For example, if S had a pain of the searing, nose-tip kind, when a burning cigarette collided with the tip of the nose of S's body (X), and if S now thinks, 'There was a searing, nose-tip pain that occurred at the time of the collision of the burning cigarette with the tip of X's nose,' then S may be said to identify a particular experience— S is justified in saying (thinking): '*the* searing nose-tip

pain that occurred at the time of the collision of the
burning cigarette with the tip of X's nose . . .' (Of
course, one may be mistaken in his beliefs about the past,
and if there was no such experience then S does not
succeed in identifying a particular experience. The possibility of this kind of error constitutes no special problem—aside from the independent-check issue, discussed
in Chapter II, with which we are not presently concerned.)

"I so use the phrases 'experiences of exactly the same
kind' and 'experience of exactly such-and-such kind' that
the former refers to qualitatively identical experiences,
and the latter expresses the idea of a complete description
of the (nondispositional and nonrelational) properties
of the experience in question. Regarding the latter, it might
be objected that it is far from clear just what it is for
the description of an experience to be complete. Granted,
but then this is true when it comes to the idea of a
complete description for most things, and this involves
no *special* problem in the case at hand.

"Why does it follow from S's inability to distinguish
his $\emptyset$ from *my* $\emptyset$ that 'it is a conceptual truth of S's
pure-experience language that no two experiences of
exactly the same kind occur at the same time'? Because,
lacking a concept of self, and, consequently, lacking a
way of identifying particular experiences of a given
kind by ascribing them to a particular person, S can
identify particular experiences only by means of the joint
specification of their dates and their exact natures. The
very idea of particular experiences is logically correlative
with the idea of their identification, and since the latter
is the only means available to S of identifying such particulars, his pure-experience language must be one in
which pure experiences are identified accordingly. The
word 'only' needs qualification: given that one can iden-

tify experiences in this way, one may sometimes identify them in other ways, for example, as 'the only pain that occurred yesterday.'

"All of this, regarding a pure-experience language (e.g., that of S at t_1), is quite compatible with the fact that particular experiences (of persons) are not identified in this way in the person language (e.g., they are not identified in this way by S at t_2). Thus, we traditionists may agree with Strawson when he says: 'A twinge of toothache or a private impression of red cannot in general be identified in our common language except as the twinge which such-and-such an identified person suffered or is suffering, the impression which such-and-such an identified person had or is having.' [9] Once again, too, it should be clear that in saying 'it is a conceptual truth of S's pure-experience language that no two experiences of exactly the same kind occur at the same time,' I was not denying, what in person language we would affirm by saying, that different persons may have qualitatively identical experiences at the same time. I was not denying this, just as in saying, from the point of view of one who speaks a pure-experience language, 'There is a certain kind of pain, $\emptyset$, when and only when the body X is in the state $\emptyset$, and similarly for other experiences and other states of X,' I was not denying, what in person language we would affirm by saying, that there is no one body upon which everyone's experiences are (empirically or causally) dependent."

[9] *Ibid.*, p. 41.

6) Further Wittgensteinian Criticism

W: "Even if you should be correct in thinking that
a pure-experience language of the sort that you defend
is possible,[10] by what right do you claim that the person
language may be 'constructed' out of a pure-experience
language? You maintain: 'Thus, a person, S, may "construct" a language in which experiences are ascribed to
persons out of a pure-experience language, in the sense
that the experiences to which the terms of the latter
refer constitute, in part, S's basis for the ascription of
experiences to persons.' You claim:

> The person language is not a PL_1. Nevertheless, the
> meanings of its experiential terms do not consist
> merely in their connections with bodily states: these
> terms designate the sorts of experiences designated by
> the terms of a pure-experience PL_1, although they re-
> fer to such experiences not as pure or unowned ex-
> periences but as the experiences *of* persons. This non-
> behavioral content of the experiential terms of the
> person language is a result of the fact that the person
> language is constructed from the more primitive pure-
> experience language.

But the experiences to which we allude in person language are such that more than one experience of exactly

[10] Cf. *ibid.*, p. 109; where Strawson appears to grant the possibility of some such language: "One might give up talking or
devise, perhaps, a different structure [than that of ordinary
language] in terms of which to soliloquize." On the other
hand, cf. p. 101 where Strawson seems to have some doubts
about this.

the same kind can occur at the same time. This is not true of the experiences to which one may refer in the pure-experience language that you advocate. The experiences alluded to in person language are, by definition, the experiences of persons. This is not true of the experiences to which one may refer in a pure-experience language. How, then, can you contend that the terms of person language designate the sorts of experiences designated by the terms of a pure-experience PL_1?"

T: "There would be no point in speaking of the construction of a person language out of a pure-experience language unless the two were different languages. That they are, indeed, different, emerges clearly from your last remarks, for you have drawn our attention to the fact that these languages have different rules. It follows from these differences in their rules that the languages involve different notions of experience. This is only to be expected, and, indeed, is implicit in my contention that the one language is constructed from the other. In what sense, then, is it true that the terms of person language 'designate the sorts of experiences designated by the terms of a pure-experience PL_1'? In the sense that, these differences notwithstanding, the experiences ascribed to persons (myself or others) in person language are in some important ways the same as those experiences formerly spoken of in pure-experience language. True, they are now to be identified by being ascribed to a particular person at a particular time rather than by their date together with their complete description. But they are to be ascribed to oneself when one would formerly have said (in pure-experience language), for example, 'There is now a $\emptyset$,' and they are to be ascribed to others when one would formerly have said (in pure-experience language), for example, 'There is an empirical correlation between ψ's and the $\emptyset$-states of body X, and the body Y is now $\emptyset$.' It is in this sense that, in person language, one talks of the sorts of experiences designated by the terms of a pure-experience PL_1. It is in this sense that person language may be said to be constructed from pure-experience language. And this is important because it means, *contra* you Wittgensteinians, that a language in which experiences are ascribed to persons need not be such that the significance of its experiential terms resides exclusively in their connections with publicly observable phenomena."

$W:$ "I wish also to ask you by what right you maintain that one who speaks a pure-experience language and not a person language (e.g., S at t_1) possesses a concept of human bodies or of any bodies whatever? Physical objects (viz., macroöbjects, not microparticles of physics), that is, bodies, and, *a fortiori,* human bodies, are, by definition, publicly observable phenomena. It is a conceptual truth that they are observable by various *persons.* Clearly, then, S can have no concept of any bodies at t_1, for at t_1 S has no concept of a person. And without a concept of bodies, he cannot have the concept of *other* bodies and consequently cannot construct the person language in the fashion you suggest."

$T:$ "Your point is well taken. It does indeed show us that, at t_1, S cannot possess the concept of physical objects that is possessed by a speaker of person language (e.g., S at t_2). But it does not follow from this that at t_1 S does not have any concept of physical objects. There is no reason why S should not employ at t_1 a concept of physical objects that is in all ways like that of person language *except* that it is not a concept of publicly observable phenomena. Why should not S single out certain patterns of experiences and refer to them as trees, human bodies, etc.? Of course, at t_2, when he has available to him a concept of persons, S may alter his original concept of physical objects so that it is a conceptual truth of his person language that physical objects are publicly observable. This he may do, just as he may alter his original concept of experiences so that it is a conceptual truth of his person language that experiences are always the experiences of persons and that two qualitatively identical experiences may occur simultaneously. Thus, I grant you that his concept of physical objects at t_1 is not the same as his concept of physical objects at t_2, just as I have admitted that his concept of experiences at t_2 differs from his concept of experiences at t_1. Nevertheless, just as there is an important sense in which he may be said to talk at t_2 about the same sorts of experiences of which he spoke at t_1, so too may he be said, in important respects, to talk at t_2 about the same sorts of physical objects of which he spoke at t_1.

"As you indicate, the concept of bodies that is possessed by a speaker of person language is not the same as the concept of bodies possessed by one who speaks a pure-experience language and not a person language. It does not follow, however, that the latter cannot possess any concept whatever of physical objects. He may possess the sort of concept of physical objects (or bodies) to which I have alluded, and he may utilize this concept in his construction of the person language. Thus, this construction is not, as you thought, impossible, even though, as you correctly perceive, at t_1 S does not possess that concept of physical objects (publicly observable phenomena) possessed by a speaker of person language.

"Indeed, now that you call the latter fact to my attention, I realize that I have granted you far too much. I granted you (in Sec. 4b) that person language cannot

be a PL$_1$ because I mistakenly supposed that a traditionist could and would use publicly observable phenomena
as well as pure experiences in constructing person language by means of the technique of the analogy argument. Now that it is clear that the bodily states that
are used in this construction cannot be publicly observable phenomena, I may properly maintain that
person language may itself be viewed as a PL$_1$ that is
not only possible but serviceable (in every sense of this
term). This PL$_1$ is to be constructed, in accordance with
the technique of the analogy argument, from pure experiences and (what is nothing but further pure experiences) bodily states, where 'bodily states' (and 'bodies'
and 'physical objects') is taken to refer to patterns of
pure experiences."

W: "You courageously try to turn defeat into victory.
For some time now you have defended the idea that
person language could be constructed from pure experiences and bodily states (in the sense of publicly
observable phenomena). When you realize that this cannot be done, you bravely say that this is all to the good,
that you will use 'bodily states' (in the sense of patterns
of pure experiences) in your construction and thereby
produce a person language that is a PL$_1$ and that is not
only possible but serviceable. I am afraid, however, that
your hopes are doomed to disappointment.

"Just as the notion of *my* experiences is conceptually
linked to the notion of *his* experiences, so the notion of
physical objects is conceptually linked to the notion of
persons who may observe such objects. Given that S
speaks pure-experience language but has no concept of
persons, you argue that S can use a notion of 'physical
objects' (or 'bodily states') to introduce the notion of
persons, where the former notion is that of patterns of

experiences rather than a notion of publicly observable phenomena. But notice that these 'physical objects' not only are not *publicly* observable, they are not observable at all by anyone: since S has no notion of persons, he can have no conception of *myself* or of *my own* observation of a physical object or of anyone's *observations* of anything at all. Does it any longer even seem plausible to suppose that S could be said to be thinking of anything remotely resembling physical objects? I think not.

"From the very beginning of our discussion you have traded on the notion of publicly observable phenomena. You have spoken of talking, of writing in diaries, of experiences occurring when a cigarette collides with a nose or when an apple falls, of correlations between charts and experiences, of inferring experiences on the basis of correlations between experiences and bodily states, and so forth. So long as it was supposed that you had a right to the notion of persons, it seemed legitimate to allow you the notion of publicly observable phenomena. But now, when you choose to put your self in the position of S (at t_1)—who has no concept of persons—in order to 'construct' person language from pure-experience language, you have no right to employ the notion of publicly observable phenomena. Indeed, you cannot utilize the concept of *myself* or anyone else *observing* anything. In this case, you cannot talk of physical objects at all."

T: "I concede that it is odd in the extreme to use 'physical object' to refer to that to which no notion of observation applies. But isn't this oddity to be expected when one departs from person language in order to try to construct this language from something else? I would maintain that the patterns of pure experiences to which I wish to refer by 'physical object' will serve in the construction of person language, and if you are troubled by this use of 'physical object,' then let us simply refer to these not as 'physical objects,' 'bodies,' etc., but as 'patterns of pure experiences.'

"It is, of course, true that I cannot properly employ 'person-laden' concepts such as *my* experiences' or '(observable) bodily states' in the construction of person language out of pure-experience language. If I am to show that person language may be viewed as logically derivative with respect to pure-experience language, I must use no person-laden concepts in defining or elucidating the notion of persons-having-experiences. Therefore, I now maintain that we traditionists can construct a PL_1 that is a person language out of a pure-experience PL_1 in such a way that talk about (observable) bodies and talk about the experiences of persons is to be elucidated exclusively in terms of pure experiences, including the patterns of pure experiences that a speaker of pure-experience language may mean to refer to by 'tree,' 'human body,' etc."

W: "We are now in a position to see that the traditionist position is thoroughly untenable. No longer will I snipe at the details of your proposed construction of person language out of pure-experience language. Rather, I shall indicate the hopeless incoherence of the idea of someone who has no notion of a person speaking a pure-experience language, and so the hopeless incoherence of the idea of a PL_1.

"It is now clear that there are only two plausible candidates for a PL_1: either a pure-experience PL_1 spoken by someone with no concept of persons, or a person language that is constructible from the latter language. Therefore, if I can show that it is impossible that someone with no concept of persons speak a pure-experience language, if I can show that this is an incoherent or senseless idea, then I shall have shown that no PL_1 is possible, that the idea of a PL_1 is a senseless or incoherent (or impossible) idea. It is this that I now wish to demonstrate.

"To do so, I must hark back to the first stage of our discussion (that of Ch. II). We there agreed that one can sensibly be said to speak a language only if he can (possibly) know that he is following the rules of his language. We agreed that a language-speaker must be able to check upon his impression that he is following a linguistic rule, that he must be able to distinguish his correctly remembering the uses to which he has put his terms from his only seeming to remember these uses. It was your contention that a PL_1-speaker can check upon his memory impressions of these matters by appeal to other memory impressions of his, by means of correlations that he has reason to believe have held within his experience, by inferences concerning these correlations. You delineated a variety of ways in which, you maintained, a PL_1-speaker could win the right to believe, could be justified in believing, that he had had certain experiences and had used certain words or signs in association with these experiences. We disagreed mainly over the question of the legitimacy of the sorts of checks that such a PL_1-speaker would employ, namely, nonindependent checks.

"Now, however, we must look at the matter anew in light of the factors that have emerged from our investigation of the issues surrounding the ascription argument. In particular, we now must view that PL_1-speaker (discussed in Ch. II) as one who has no concept of persons and yet who is supposed to speak a pure-experience PL_1. But as soon as we do this, it should be clear that this hypothetical person could not possibly be said to speak a language, that is, his supposed PL_1 could not possibly be a language. Why not? Well, remember that he has no concept of persons and so no concept of *myself* or *my* experiences. In this case, how can he sensibly be said to speak a language? Can he say (think), 'I know I am following the rules of my language'? Can he say (think), 'I've checked up on this memory impression of mine and found that some others with which it conflicts are correct'? Can he say (think), 'I seem to remember a twinge of pain'? Can he say (think), 'I infer this from that,' 'I have evidence for this,' 'I don't believe that,' 'I am justified in thinking (have the epistemic right to belive) this'? The obvious answer to all of these questions is No. Without a concept of persons, and hence of *myself*, the putative PL_1-speaker cannot sensibly be said to be involved in checking, remembering, believing, inferring, knowing, weighing evidence, etc. But then he cannot sensibly be said to check upon his linguistic practice or to have a linguistic practice. He cannot sensibly be said to speak a language.

"The very defenses that for so long enabled you to stand off my assaults (in both Ch. II and Ch. III) are defenses to which you had no right. This fact becomes fully apparent, however, only when it is seen that you can defend the private object, that is, the idea of a PL_1, only if you can defend the idea of a pure-experience language spoken by one who has no concept of *myself* or any self. In the early stages of our discussion (Chs. II and III), it seemed proper for you to utilize the defenses that you employed. Thus, you maintained (in Ch. II) that the PL_1-speaker can *remember* that he has *used* his terms correctly (in accordance with a rule), that he is *justified* in *believing* (has an epistemic *right* to believe) this, that he can *know* that he *speaks* a PL_1. But the entire discussion of those issues presupposed that the traditionist has a concept of *myself* and *my* experiential data. This presupposition has no application in the case of one who speaks a pure-experience language and not a person language. This person cannot think of remembering (or seeming to remember), of being justified, (of having an epistemic right), of believing, of knowing, etc.—for he can think of no person doing any of these or being in such a state, and thus he cannot think of himself in these ways. Indeed, he cannot think of language, even private language, for he cannot think of a person and so cannot think of himself or anyone else speaking a language, following a rule, using terms correctly (or incorrectly).

"If he has no concept of persons, a speaker of pure-experience language cannot know (or think) anything about languages, public or private, or about experiences or about physical objects of any kind; for he will have no concept of language, no concept of justification, belief, knowledge, evidence, etc. You proposed and accepted the testability principle (in Ch. III), for example, in accordance with which an utterance is a meaningful (synthetic) statement only if it is possible to have evidence for it and evidence against it. But one who speaks a pure-experience language and who has no concept of a person will have no concept of evidence. It seems clear that the very idea of such a person thinking, or speaking a language, has been reduced to nonsense. Yet it has become manifest that it is this idea upon which the entire traditionist position, the defense of the private object, is based.

"You may imagine that we can make sense of this idea if we think of such a person's speaking a pure-experience language as something that *we*, who speak person language, can think about and find out about. But this is to construct the private object (PL_1) out of public objects (public language) rather than vice versa. It is the impossible task of building the notion of private objects (objects that are conceptually independent of publicly observable phenomena) out of notions that are themselves conceptually dependent upon public objects (objects that are conceptually dependent upon publicly observable phenomena). In the end, then, the idea of a private language makes no sense."

T: "I must admit that you seem to be correct. Again and again in the course of our discussion, I have assumed that an alleged PL_1-speaker was remembering, checking, inferring, justifying, knowing, speaking, etc. Only now do I see that I had no right to such assumptions. As long as it appeared legitimate to suppose the PL_1-speaker to possess the concept of *myself,* these assumptions seemed quite innocuous, as did the assumption that the speaker could speak or think of physical objects. Only now does the full import of the idea of the private object strike me. Now I see that these assumptions can have no application to one who has no concept of persons, indeed, that without a concept of persons one could not be said to speak a language at all. I had thought that the idea of a person language that is itself a PL_1 could be elucidated in terms of a pure-experience PL_1. Now I realize that the former is impossible, because one who lacks the concept of persons could not possibly speak a pure-experience PL_1. It seems clear, then, that a PL_1 is impossible.

"Nevertheless, it remains hard to believe that there is nothing at all to the idea of the private object. Can it really be that there is nothing to the pains I feel except all of the behavior and physical conditions that are evidentially relevant to my pains? This is difficult, indeed, to swallow."

W: "Let me remind you (cf. Ch. I, Sec. 3d) that we Wittgensteinians do not deny that people *feel* pains, that they actually *suffer* with them, etc. We do not deny the existence of experiential data, nor do we try to reduce them to something else such as behavior. You want to ask, ' "But you will surely admit that there is a difference between pain-behaviour accompanied by pain and pain-behaviour without any pain?" ' (*Inv.,* 304). Wittgenstein's response is unequivocal: 'Admit it? What greater difference could there be?' (*ibid.*). '*Certainly* all these things happen in you.—And now all I ask is to understand the expression we use' (*Inv.,* 423). We only endeavor to reveal the logic of the language of experiences and to expose the welter of confusions that tempt one to misconstrue the logic of this language. Surely there is no more tempting and important delusion in this regard than the chimera of a private language.

"It would be a mistake to allow the importance of bodily states in the language of experiences to lead us to insist that 'I am in pain' is not a statement but a cry, or that it means or is about behavior. As Malcolm points out, when Wittgenstein maintains that 'I am in pain' is an 'expression' of pain, 'Wittgenstein *stretches ordinary language* and in so doing illuminates the hidden continuity between the utterance of that sentence and— expressions of pain.' [11] As Strawson indicates, it is an

---

[11] Malcolm, "Wittgenstein's *Philosophical Investigations,*" *op. cit.,* p. 111 (our italics); cf. pp. 106–11, 117–22; also cf. Malcolm, "Knowledge of Other Minds," *Knowledge and Certainty, op. cit.,* p. 140.

error '. . . to think that all there is in the meaning of . . . [psychological] predicates is the criteria on the strength of which we ascribe them to others.' " [12]

T: "Well, what more is there in the meaning of psychological predicates such as 'pain'? If there is something more, mustn't it be a private something?"

W: "These questions of yours are but another expression of the urge behind the very confusions over private language that we have been exploring all along. You continue to quest after an entity, a stuff, a something, of which you can say, '*This* is what pain really is.' But to concentrate upon your pain when you are in pain and say, '*This* is what pain really is' is philosophically idle: of course, this is what pain is, since you are in pain. It is also philosophically dangerous: for it tempts you to think that introspection can give you the meaning of 'pain.' A search of this kind can never uncover a solution to your puzzle (cf. *Inv.*, 304–16). Instead, we must say with Wittgenstein, '*this language-game is played*,'[13] and we must study the way that it is played. This study will, of course, reveal the fact that it is a gross oversimplification of the language-game of experiences to claim that there is nothing to the experiences I have except all of the behavior and physical conditions that are evidentially relevant to my experiences (cf. Ch. IV, Sec. 4b). But this does not mean that there must be a something, an entity, a stuff—be it private or public—that somehow constitutes the real meaning of experiential words. Rather it means that the meaning of experiential terms consists in their place

[12] Strawson, *op. cit.*, p. 110.
[13] *Inv.*, 654. Cf. *Inv.*, 654–55.

in the language-game of experiences, in the uses to which we put them, and thus in the complex of rules and practices that involve the use of these terms. There is no place in this complex for private objects; but this does not mean that there is no place in this complex for experiences. There is: pains, for example, are experiences; and the events and processes of being in pain do occur; and it is such nonprivate events and processes that we talk about when we talk about our experiences and the experiences of others. Pain is not behavior or physical evidence, but neither is it a private substance. In making a study of the language-game of experiences, we shall, of course, note that we do indeed have pains, that we can tell others about them, and that we do not report our pains to others on the basis of physical evidence. But then we knew this all along, didn't we?"

V |
Conclusion

It is time to assess the results of our investigation. The results of Chapters II and III were highly inconclusive. It was not until the end of Chapter IV that it was definitively established that a PL_1 is impossible, that is, that the idea of the private object is an incoherent notion. We wish here to review in bald outline the course of the foregoing debate between W and T, and to indicate why it should be so that such a conclusive result could emerge only after a consideration of the material of Chapter IV.

In Chapter II we examined the question whether a person might speak a PL_1 even if this language were necessarily a PL_2. For this purpose it was assumed that a PL_1 could not be understood by anyone other than its speaker. On the basis of this assumption, W contended that since T could not possibly avail himself of the testimony of other persons in order to check upon his memory impressions regarding his experiential data, T could not even be said to have such memory impressions. T admitted that he could not make use of such checks, but he denied that he could use no checks at all. In particular, T argued that although he could not have *independent* checks upon his memory impressions of private objects, he nevertheless could employ nonindependent checks and that these were good enough. T allowed that if he could not check upon his memory impressions of his experiences, then it would make no sense to say that he had such experiences, that he spoke of them, or that he had memory impressions of them: that his PL_1 would indeed be impossible if he could not check upon his impression that he was following this or that rule of the language. He insisted, however, that he could do this by means of nonindependent checks, by means of checks whose evidential value ultimately rested upon nothing other than his own memory impressions. Thus, W denied, and T affirmed, the legitimacy of nonindependent checks.

There, for the time being, the matter had to rest. W insisted that nonindependent checks are not really checks, but T emphatically disagreed. T maintained that the logic of his PL_1 neither permits nor requires independent checks and that it is none the worse for that. When W argued that publicity is essential to the notion of a check, T countered that these arguments were tantamount to the impossible demand that a private language conform to the standards of public language. He accused W of intolerance, of linguistic inflexibility. No matter how sympathetic one might be to the frustrations of W, it does seem that this stage of the debate reaches stalemate at this point. It does appear that T and W have different conceptions of checks and of language and that it would be somewhat arbitrary to insist that terms such as "rule," "check," and "language," be used only in W's way and not in T's way. At this stage, it does seem to shed more heat than light to label *impossible* or *senseless* the alleged traditionist language: thus, we were led to suggest that resolution of the disagreement might require more a change in attitude than a change of opinion regarding matters of fact. Surely, the basic disagreement over the *legitimacy* of nonindependent checks must involve a valuational or an attitudinal component of some significance.

The results of Chapter III were, similarly, inconclusive, and for much the same sorts of reasons. W maintained that a PL_1 is necessarily a PL_2, that, on the traditionist position, no one can know the mind of another. T denied this, appealing to the analogy argument regarding other minds. W argued that the analogy argument is illegitimate (for a traditionist), because a traditionist cannot test the conclusions of such arguments except by means of more arguments of the same kind. T conceded that the analogy argument allows of no independent tests, but he insisted that it is nonetheless legitimate. When W contended that for a traditionist the experiences of other persons are ineffable "beetles in boxes," T admitted that they have the epistemic status of beetles in boxes but refused to agree that they are therefore ineffable. Once again the dispute between W and T had moved to the point of stalemate. Once more we found T affirming and W denying the legitimacy of a mode of justification, in this case the legitimacy of the analogy argument. Again it was the nonindependence of the mode of justification espoused by T that lay at the nub of the disagreement. Once more it seemed that only some change in attitude could resolve the dispute: a dispute in which T insisted that his language does not require the independent testability of the analogy argument as a condition of its legitimacy, while W replied that this only reveals that a PL_1 is necessarily a PL_2, that a traditionist cannot meaningfully talk of the mind of another person. It is tempting, indeed, to characterize the traditionist's position as Malcolm did:

> "That there should be thinking or pain other than my own is unintelligible," he ought to hold. This would be a rigorous solipsism, and a correct outcome of the assumption that one can know only from one's own case what the mental phenomena are. An equivalent way of putting it would be: "When I say 'I am in pain,' by 'pain' I mean a certain inward state. When I say '*He* is in pain,' by 'pain' I mean *behavior*. I cannot attribute pain to others *in the same sense* that I attribute it to myself." [1]

For T admitted that although he utilizes the *behavior* of others in order to learn of their experiences, he can never check upon the conclusions he draws in any way other than by appeal to more of their *behavior*. It may be best, however, to resist this temptation at this stage of the argument. In saying that the analogy argument (and the traditionist language that embodies it) is illegitimate or senseless, one is, at least in part, making a value judgment. It is proper to doubt whether W was not, in part at least, simply turning up his nose at a language-game that differs considerably from those that he would view with approbation. Unless it were even clearer than, in fact, it seemed to be at the close of

---

[1] N. Malcolm, "Knowledge of Other Minds," *Knowledge and Certainty: Essays and Lectures* (Englewood Cliffs, N.J.: Prentice-Hall, Inc., 1963), p. 137.

Chapter III that it was not linguistic preference but the power of logic that led W to repudiate the analogy argument, it ought not to be concluded that the argument cannot possibly work and that a PL_1 is necessarily a PL_2.

In Chapter IV, however, the noose tightens as the considerations of Chapters II and III are combined with the ascription argument to produce an argument that we think does succeed in establishing the impossibility of a PL_1 (of the private object).

The ascription argument shows that the concept of *my* experiences cannot be treated as logically primitive with respect to the concept of *his* experiences (the experiences of *other* persons): if one has no concept of other persons, one has no concept of persons, and so no concept of *my*self or *my* experiences. Hence, a traditionist cannot commence from his own case (*my own* experiences) in order either to infer or to construct the experiences of other persons. Nor can he "begin" with the experiences of others in addition to his own: for a traditionist cannot construe the logic of "*his* experiences" in terms of the one thing about other persons that could be available to him as evidence, namely, their behavior (or bodily states). This being so, there are only two plausible alternatives open to a traditionist: either he maintains that person language (talk about persons having experiences) is (or may be construed as) a PL_1, the logic of which can be elucidated in terms of a pure-experience PL_1, or else he maintains that it is, at any rate, possible for one who has no concept of a person to speak a pure-experience PL_1. Since the first alternative can succeed only if the second alternative can succeed, in order to demonstrate the impossibility of a PL_1, it is sufficient to demonstrate that it is impossible for one who has no concept of persons to speak a pure-experience language. Thus, if it can be shown that a pure-experience PL_1 spoken by someone who has no concept of a person is impossible, it will have been shown that any PL_1, be it a person language or a pure-experience language, is impossible.

And this can be shown: Let S be a traditionist who has no concept of a person. S cannot think of himself as believing, knowing, remembering, seeming to remember, inferring, being justified in believing, having evidence, checking, following rules, speaking correctly (or incorrectly), or speaking a language at all. But then he could hardly be said to do or be involved in any of these things. Could he do (or be involved in) such things and yet not know, be unconscious of, not realize this? Hardly. These are not that sort of thing. (A *dog* can *dig for* a bone and, of course, does not know that it is doing so, but a *person* cannot *check, weigh evidence,* etc., without realizing that he is doing so.) There may be some temptation to shrug off this point and to suggest that S might somehow be following the rules of his language, even though he has no idea that he is doing this. But that is not what is meant by *following* rules. There may be some temptation, nevertheless, to say that this will serve as an odd case of following rules —that it is at least possible that this is going on, that even if S has no idea what he is doing, *we* (who have the concept of persons) can know that this is going on. But, for one thing, as just indicated, a mere correlation between "signs" and pure experiences (or anything else) is not a case, not even an odd case, of following rules. Further, to rest the possibility of S's pure-experience PL_1 upon the possibility of other persons (who have the concept of persons) knowing about this, is to explain the idea of a pure-experience PL_1 in terms of person language. It is to abandon the attempt to explain the public in terms of the private. It is to pretend that one is still dealing with the private while introducing the supposedly private in terms of public phenomena.

The foregoing line of argument demolishes the idea of the private object (or PL_1). Thus, the traditionist of our dialogue conceded defeat at the end. It is interesting and important to understand that *resounding* defeat could come only at the end of Chapter IV, that is, only when the Wittgensteinian attacks of Chapters II and III were combined with the ascription argument of Chapter IV. So long as the traditionist is permitted a concept of *myself* and *my* experiences, the arguments against him remain less than overwhelming. He can maintain, as did T in Chapters II and III, that he is obeying the rules of his private language, and that while these differ considerably from the rules of a public language, they are rules nonetheless. He can maintain that his is not a public language, but it is a language nonetheless. He can accuse the Wittgensteinian of linguistic bias, of philosophical favoritism, of a prejudice in behalf of the public. Since the P-L problem is a very basic, or root-level, philosophical matter, it is not easy to dispose of such accusations: it is somewhat unconvincing to rule out as impossible or senseless what seem to be alternative language-games. The idea of the private language-game appeals to us all as an idea of which we, perhaps, ought to be tolerant, as an idea that may have something in it even though it deviates from the idea of the public language-game. It is only with the advent of the ascription argument that T is deprived of the foregoing escape from the early attacks of Chapters II and III: only then is this exit sealed off.

One way of putting the matter is this: The traditionist can dodge the attacks of Chapters II and III by

maintaining that he is following the rules of a language
that has a rather unique logic. He can dodge the ascription argument of Chapter IV by shifting his ground
to talk of *pure* experiences. There is no room left, no
place to turn, however, when he is caught between the
earlier and the later attacks. The earlier attacks force
him to admit that he must live up to rules, that he
must be able to check upon his impression that he is
doing so, that he must be able to have evidence for his
contentions regarding private objects. The later attack,
the ascription argument, compels him to discard the
notions of *myself* and *my* experiences in order to defend the private status that he claims for these experiences. But then, bereft of a notion of *myself*, or of
any persons, he cannot be said to live up to rules, to
check—in a word, to speak a language. Neither the
earlier nor the later assaults, by themselves, quite man-
age to overcome traditionism. But together they van-
quish it utterly.

Still, it may be objected, and with good point, that
a PL_1 is possible despite all that we have said. For "a
PL_1" has been defined as: a language each word of
which refers to experiential data, although each of these
words is conceptually independent of publicly observable phenomena. And "conceptual independence" has
been so defined that "An experiential-datum term, 'E,'
is conceptually independent of publicly observable phenomena" means: the existence of an E neither entails
nor is entailed by the existence of any publicly observable phenomena; nor is it part of the meaning of
"E" that publicly observable phenomena provide evidence for the existence of an E. Now suppose that there
is a person, S, who has a concept of persons and a concept of publicly observable phenomena and who also
has a concept (that is not a PL_1-concept) of persons-

having-experiences: S has at his disposal a number of experiential-datum terms that are not PL_1-terms (i.e., that are not conceptually independent of publicly observable phenomena), which he can use to ascribe *non*-private experiences to persons. In this case, why could not S *also* have at his disposal a number of *other* experiential-datum terms that *are* PL_1-terms (i.e., that are conceptually independent of publicly observable phenomena), which he can use to ascribe *private* experiences to persons? For example, suppose that S one day has a sensation, G, that is different from any of the sensations that he refers to with his non-PL_1-terms. Could he not keep a record (using the new term "G") of the various G-sensations that he has during (say) April? Could he not find that these G-sensations have been correlated with certain of his bodily states, and could he not then inductively infer that another person is having a G when he finds another person to be in a bodily state of the same kind? In this case, there are (as yet, anyhow) no *criteria* (no bodily states that count as *direct* evidence) for the existence of G's. Yet S, who has a concept of persons-having-experiences, can ascribe G's to himself and to others. We think that it was the possibility of situations like this that Strawson had in mind when he said:

And, in the case of *at least some* P-predicates [i.e., roughly, psychological predicates], the ways of telling must constitute in some sense logically adequate kinds of criteria for the ascription of the P-predicate.[2]
There is no sense in the idea of ascribing states of consciousness to oneself, or at all, unless the ascriber already knows how to ascribe *at least some* states of

[2] P. F. Strawson, *Individuals: An Essay in Descriptive Metaphysics* (London: Methuen and Co. Ltd., 1965), p. 105 (our italics).

consciousness to others. So he cannot argue *in general* "from his own case" to conclusions about how to do this. . . .[3]

According to our definitions (rehearsed above) of "PL_1" and "conceptual independence," terms such as "G" will be PL_1-terms, and if S can use some terms of this sort then these terms will constitute a PL_1. In this case and in this way, a PL_1 is, indeed, possible. But it must also be noted that this is an *attenuated* kind of PL_1: such a group of PL_1-terms is possible only in connection with a language that contains the concepts of persons, physical objects, and, most notably, that contains experiential-datum terms that are not the private terms of a PL_1 but are conceptually dependent upon publicly observable phenomena. Such a PL_1 is therefore *parasitic* upon public language. This attenuated kind of PL_1 is possible only in virtue of our (above rehearsed) definitions of "PL_1" and "conceptual independence." And these are restrictive definitions, narrow rather than broad, that facilitate the defense of private language: for they permit the words of a PL_1 to be conceptually related to publicly observable phenomena in ways other than those specified in these definitions.

Thus, we could easily and justifiably redefine "PL_1" in such a way as to preclude the possibility of even this parasitic sort of PL_1. We could redefine "PL_1" to mean: a language each word of which refers to experiential data, although each of these words is *only contingently* related to publicly observable phenomena.[4] In this case,

[3] *Ibid.*, p. 106 (our italics).
[4] Phenomenalistic traditionists attempt to elucidate the meaning of physical-object expressions in terms of the words of a PL_1. Therefore such traditionists presumably would wish to qualify this redefinition of "PL_1" by specifying that although there may be noncontingent relations between PL_1-words and

the group of terms considered above would not qualify as a PL_1: since it is only in virtue of S's ability to use *other* experiential-datum terms that *are* conceptually dependent upon publicly observable phenomena that S is able to use experiential-datum terms, like "G," that are not conceptually dependent upon publicly observable phenomena. So if private objects are possible at all, they are possible only in an attenuated and restrictive sense (of "private object") in which they are in an important way *non*private, being parasitic upon public objects, namely, *non*private experiential data and publicly observable phenomena.[5]

_____

publicly observable phenomena, these relations may obtain *only* in virtue of the PL_1-words serving in the definition or analysis of expressions that refer to\publicly observable phenomena—so that a PL_1 is in no way parasitic upon physical objects or any publicly observable phenomena. For the reasons we have rehearsed, this sort of PL_1 is impossible.

[5] Malcolm and Wittgenstein would not concede even this much to the defender of the private object. They hold that the considerations adduced by *W* in Chapters II and III suffice to topple the notion of the private object. These considerations focus on the point that a PL_1-speaker could not have independent checks upon his alleged ascriptions of experiences to himself or to others. And this point applies, as well, to one who speaks an attenuated PL_1 of the kind depicted above: this speaker has no *criteria* for the application of his PL_1-terms, and so can have no independent checks upon his impressions regarding his uses of these terms. If we are correct in thinking, *contra* Wittgenstein and Malcolm, that such attenuated private objects are possible, then the Wittgensteinian dictum, "An 'inner process' stands in need of outward criteria" (*Inv.*, 580), ought to be qualified to mean that *some significant number of* inner processes, rather than *all* inner processes, must have outward criteria.

SELECTED
BIBLIOGRAPHY

The following list is comprised of references to books and articles of three sorts: those in which PL is the main theme, those that deal with PL in connection with some other topic, and those that bear tangentially upon the P-L problem. Inclusion or exclusion of an item from the last category is somewhat arbitrary, but we have tried to make listings falling under the first and second headings as complete as possible. Although we do not distinguish these three sorts of entries from one another in our bibliography, the title of a book or an article will usually indicate its relevance to the P-L problem. In the case of books and some articles, however, whenever feasible we have included references to places where material concerning PL occurs.

As we remarked in Chapter I, Section 1, of this book, explicit recognition of the P-L problem is confined to the twentieth century. We have therefore omitted from this bibliography references to works of predominantly historical significance, except those cited in the text. In pre-twentieth-century literature, the concept of a PL is implicit only and, more often than not, presupposed in scattered passages throughout works of considerable length.

When articles have appeared in more than one place, the page references in our footnotes refer to the first place cited in any given bibliographic listing.

Abelson, R. "Persons, P-Predicates, and Robots," *American Philosophical Quarterly*, III (Oct., 1966).

Albritton, R. "On Wittgenstein's Use of the Term 'Criterion,'" *Journal of Philosophy*, LVI (Oct. 22, 1959).

Anscombe, G. E. M. *An Introduction to Wittgenstein's Tractatus*. London: Hutchinson and Co. Ltd., 1959. Esp. pp. 138–39, 167.

———. *Intention*. Oxford: Basil Blackwell, 1958. Cf. Sec. 18.

Armstrong, D. M. "Is Introspective Knowledge Incorrigible?" *Philosophical Review*, LXXII (Oct., 1963).

Aune, B. "Feelings, Moods, and Introspection," *Mind*, LXXII (April, 1963).

———. "Feigl on the Mind-Body Problem," in P. K. Feyerabend and G. Maxwell, eds., *Mind, Matter, and Method: Essays in Honor of Herbert Feigl*. Minneapolis: University of Minnesota Press, 1966.

———. "Knowing and Merely Thinking," *Philosophical Studies*, XII (June, 1961).

———. *Knowledge, Mind, and Nature*. New York: Random House, 1967.

———. "On the Complexity of Avowals," in M. Black, ed., *Philosophy in America*. Ithaca, N.Y.: Cornell University Press, 1965.

———. "On Thought and Feeling," *Philosophical Quarterly*, XIII (Jan., 1963).

———. "The Problem of Other Minds," *Philosophical Review*, LXX (July, 1961).

Ayer, A. J. "Can There Be a Private Language?" (symposium); repr., with additional footnotes, in Ayer, *The Concept of a Person and Other Essays*. London: Macmillan and Co. Ltd., 1963. Orig. in *Proceedings of the Aristotelian Society*, Suppl. XXVIII (1954).

———. "Carnap's Treatment of the Problem of Other Minds," in P. A. Schilpp, ed., *The Philosophy of Rudolf Carnap*. La Salle, Ill.: Open Court Publishing Co., 1963.

———. "The Concept of a Person," *The Concept of a Person and Other Essays*. London: Macmillan and Co. Ltd., 1963.

————. *The Foundations of Empirical Knowledge.* London: Macmillan and Co. Ltd., 1940. Cf. Ch. III.

————. *Language, Truth and Logic.* London: Victor Gollancz Ltd., 1936; 2nd ed., 1946. See pp. 10–11, 18–20, 90–94; Ch. VII.

————. "Other Minds," *Proceedings of the Aristotelian Society,* Suppl. XX (1946); repr. in Ayer, *Philosophical Essays.* London: Macmillan and Co. Ltd., 1954.

————. "Privacy," *Proceedings of the British Academy,* XLV (1959); repr. in Ayer, *The Concept of a Person and Other Essays.* London: Macmillan and Co. Ltd., 1963.

————. *The Problem of Knowledge.* Harmondsworth: Penguin Books, 1956. Cf. Chs. II and V, esp. pp. 52–61, 199–222.

————. "Professor Malcolm on Dreams," *Journal of Philosophy,* LVII (Aug. 4, 1960).

————. "Rejoinder to Professor Malcolm," *Journal of Philosophy,* LVIII (May 25, 1961).

Baier, K. "Pains," *Australasian Journal of Philosophy,* XL (May, 1962). Esp. Pt. 4.

Barnes, W. H. F. "Talking about Sensations," *Proceedings of the Aristotelian Society,* LIV (1953–1954).

Basson, A. H. "The Immortality of the Soul," *Mind,* LVIV (Jan., 1950).

Bennett, J. *Kant's Analytic.* Cambridge: Cambridge University Press, 1966. Cf. Secs. 14 and 51–2.

————. " 'Real,' " *Mind,* LXXV (Oct., 1966). Cf. p. 513.

Berkeley, G. *Works.* A. A. Luce and T. E. Jessop, eds.; vols. I and II. Edinburgh: Nelson, 1948, 1949.

Bird, G. *Kant's Theory of Knowledge: An Outline of One Central Argument in the "Critique of Pure Reason."* New York: Humanities Press, 1962. Cf. pp. 80–81, 126–36, 145–48, 166–88.

Black, M. *A Companion to Wittgenstein's "Tractatus."* Ithaca, N.Y.: Cornell University Press, 1964.

Bouwsma, O. K. "The Blue Book," *Journal of Philosophy,* LVIII (March 16, 1961).

Bradley, M. C. "Mr. Strawson and Skepticism," *Analysis,* XX (Oct., 1959).

Braybrooke, D. "Personal Beliefs without Private Languages," *Review of Metaphysics,* XVI (June, 1963).

Buck, R. C. "Non-other Minds," R. J. Butler, ed., *Analytical Philosophy.* First Series. New York: Barnes and Noble, Inc., 1962.

Carnap, R. "A. J. Ayer on Other Minds," in P. A. Schilpp, ed., *The Philosophy of Rudolf Carnap.* La Salle, Ill.: Open Court Publishing Co., 1963.

————. "Psychology in Physical Language," in A. J. Ayer, ed., *Logical Positivism*. Glencoe, Ill.: Free Press, 1959.

————. *The Unity of Science*. M. Black, trans. Psyche Miniatures, General Series No. 63. London: Kegan Paul, Trench, Trubner, and Co. Ltd., 1934.

Carney, J. D. "Private Language: The Logic of Wittgenstein's Argument," *Mind*, LXIX (Oct., 1960).

Castañeda, H. N. Abstract of "Private Languages and Third-Person Psychological Statements," *Journal of Philosophy*, LIX (Oct. 25, 1962).

————. "Criteria, Analogy, and Knowledge of Other Minds," *Journal of Philosophy*, LIX (Sept. 27, 1962).

————. "Knowledge and Certainty," *The Review of Metaphysics*, XVIII (March, 1965).

————. "The Private-Language Argument" (symposium), in C. D. Rollins, ed., *Knowledge and Experience*. Pittsburgh: University of Pittsburgh Press, 1964.

————. "Private Language Problem," in P. Edwards, ed., *The Encyclopedia of Philosophy*. New York: Crowell-Collier & Macmillan, 1967.

————. "Rejoinders" to "Comments" by V. C. Chappell and J. F. Thomson in C. D. Rollins, ed., *Knowledge and Experience*. Pittsburgh: University of Pittsburgh Press, 1964.

Chappell, V. C. "Comments" on Castañeda, "The Private-Language Argument," in C. D. Rollins, ed., *Knowledge and Experience*. Pittsburgh: University of Pittsburgh Press, 1964.

————. "The Concept of Dreaming," *Philosophical Quarterly*, XIII (July, 1963). Cf. pp. 197–205.

————. "Introduction," in V. C. Chappell, ed., *The Philosophy of Mind*. Englewood Cliffs, N.J.: Prentice-Hall, 1962.

————. "Myself and Others," *Analysis*, XXIII, Suppl. (Jan., 1963).

Chihara, C. S., and J. A. Fodor. "Operationalism and Ordinary Language: A Critique of Wittgenstein," *American Philosophical Quarterly*, II (Oct., 1965). Esp. Pt. 9.

Cohen, L. J. *The Diversity of Meaning*. New York: Herder and Herder, 1963. Cf. pp. 59–67.

Cook, J. W. "Wittgenstein on Privacy," *Philosophical Review*, LXXIV (July, 1965).

Cornman, J. W. "Private Languages and Private Entities." Paper read at the meeting of the American Philosophical Association, Western Division, May 6, 1966.

Coval, S. C. "Persons and Criteria in Strawson," *Philosophy and Phenomenological Research*, XXIV (March, 1964).

————. *Scepticism and The First Person*. London: Methuen and Co. Ltd., 1966.

Cowan, J. L. "Publicity," *Analysis*, XXVI (Oct., 1965).

Danto, A. "Nietzsche," in D. J. O'Connor, ed., *A Critical History of Western Philosophy*. New York: Free Press of Glencoe, 1964. Cf. p. 391.

Descartes, R. *Meditations on First Philosophy*, in *Philosophical Writings*. E. Anscombe and P. T. Geach, trans. Edinburgh: Nelson, 1954.

Donagan, A. "Wittgenstein on Sensation," in G. Pitcher, ed., *Wittgenstein: The Philosophical Investigations*. Garden City, N.Y.: Doubleday, 1966.

Duggan, T. "The Privacy of Experience," *Philosophical Quarterly*, XIII (April, 1963).

Farrell, B. A. "Experience," *Mind*, LIX (April, 1950).

Feigl, H. "The 'Mental' and the 'Physical,'" in H. Feigl and M. Scriven, eds., *Minnesota Studies in the Philosophy of Science*. Vol. II. Minneapolis: University of Minnesota Press, 1958.

———. "Other Minds and the Egocentric Predicament," *Journal of Philosophy*, LV (Nov. 6, 1958).

———. "Physicalism, Unity of Science and the Foundations of Psychology," in P. A. Schilpp, ed., *The Philosophy of Rudolf Carnap*. La Salle, Ill.: Open Court Publishing Co., 1963.

Feyerabend, P. "Wittgenstein's *Philosophical Investigations*," *Philosophical Review*, LXIV (July, 1955).

Findlay, J. N. "Recommendations Regarding the Language of Introspection," *Philosophy and Phenomenological Research*, IX (Dec., 1948).

———. Review of *Philosophical Investigations*, *Philosophy*, XXX (April, 1955); repr. in Findlay, *Language, Mind and Value*. London: George Allen and Unwin, 1963.

———. "Some Reactions to Recent Cambridge Philosophy," repr. in Findlay, *Language, Mind and Value*. London: George Allen and Unwin, 1963. Orig. in *Australasian Journal of Philosophy*, XVIII (Dec., 1940); XIX (April, 1941).

———. "Wittgenstein's *Philosophical Investigations*," *Revue Internationale de Philosophie*, VII, Fasc. iii, No. 25 (1953).

Flew, A. *Hume's Philosophy of Belief*. New York: Humanities Press, 1961. Cf. Ch. II.

Forrest, T. "P-Predicates," in A. Stroll, ed., *Epistemology, New Essays in the Theory of Knowledge*. New York: Harper & Row, 1967.

Garver, N. "Privacy in Grammar and Metaphysics." Paper read at the meeting of the American Philosophical Association, Western Division, May 6, 1966.

———. "Rejoinders" to "Comments" by C. Ginet, F. A. Siegler, and P. Ziff, in C. D. Rollins, ed., *Knowledge and*

Experience. Pittsburgh: University of Pittsburgh Press, 1964.

———. "Wittgenstein on Criteria" (symposium), in C. D. Rollins, ed., *Knowledge and Experience*. Pittsburgh: University of Pittsburgh Press, 1964.

———. "Wittgenstein on Private Language," *Philosophy and Phenomenological Research*, XX (March, 1960).

Gasking, D. "Avowals" (symposium), in R. J. Butler, ed., *Analytical Philosophy*. First Series. New York: Barnes and Noble, Inc., 1962.

Geach, P. T. *Mental Acts: Their Content and Their Objects*. London: Routledge and Kegan Paul, 1957.

Gert, B. "Imagination and Verifiability," *Philosophical Studies*, XVI (April, 1965).

———. "Wittgenstein and Private Language." Paper read at the meeting of the American Philosophical Association, Eastern Division, Dec. 28, 1964.

Ginet, C. "Comments" on Garver, "Wittgenstein on Criteria," in C. D. Rollins, ed., *Knowledge and Experience*. Pittsburgh: University of Pittsburgh Press, 1964.

Griffiths, A. P. "Ayer on Perception," *Mind*, LXIX (Oct., 1960). Esp. pp. 497–98.

———. "On Belief," *Proceedings of the Aristotelian Society*, LXIII (1962–1963).

Hallie, P. "The Privacy of Experience," *Journal of Philosophy*, LVIII (June 22, 1961).

Hamlyn, D. *Sensation and Perception: A History of the Philosophy of Perception*. London: Routledge and Kegan Paul, 1961. Esp. pp. 174–81.

Hampshire, S. N. "The Analogy of Feeling," *Mind*, LXI (Jan., 1952).

———. *Thought and Action*. London: Chatto and Windus, 1959. See esp. Ch. I.

Hanson, N. R. "On Having the Same Visual Experiences," *Mind*, LXIX (July, 1960).

Hardin, C. L. "Wittgenstein on Private Languages," *Journal of Philosophy*, LVI (June 4, 1959).

Heath, P. L. "Wittgenstein Investigated," *Philosophical Quarterly*, VI (Jan., 1956).

Hervey, H. "The Private Language Problem," *Philosophical Quarterly*, VII (Jan., 1957).

Hoffman, R. "Logic, Meaning, and Mystical Intuition," *Philosophical Studies*, XI (Oct., 1960).

Holland, R. F. "The Empiricist Theory of Memory," *Mind*, LXIII (Oct., 1954).

Hume, D. *A Treatise of Human Nature*. L. A. Selby-Bigge, ed. Oxford: Clarendon Press, 1888.

Hungerland, I. C. "My Pains and Yours," in A. Stroll, ed., *Epistemology, New Essays in the Theory of Knowledge.* New York: Harper & Row, 1967.

Iseminger, G. "Meaning, Criteria, and P-Predicates," *Analysis,* XXIV (Oct., 1963).

Jones, J. R. "Self-Knowledge," *Proceedings of the Aristotelian Society,* Suppl. XXX (1956).

———. "The Two Contexts of Mental Concepts," *Proceedings of the Aristotelian Society,* LIX (1958–1959).

Jones, R. I. "A Note on Ayer's No-Ownership Theory," *Philosophical Quarterly,* XV (July, 1965).

Joske, W. D. "Inferring and Perceiving," *Philosophical Review,* LXXII (Oct., 1963).

———. *Material Objects.* New York: St. Martin's Press, 1967.

Kenny, A. *Action, Emotion and Will.* London: Routledge and Kegan Paul, 1963. Cf. Chs. I–III, esp. pp. 13 and 62–75.

———. "Cartesian Privacy," in G. Pitcher, ed., *Wittgenstein: The Philosophical Investigations.* Garden City, N.Y.: Doubleday, 1966.

King-Farlow, J. "Postscript to Mr. Aune on a Wittgensteinian Dogma," *Philosophical Studies,* XIII (June, 1962).

Kneale, W. "Leibniz and the Picture Theory of Language," *Revue Internationale de Philosophie,* XX, Fasc. 2–3, No. 76–77 (1966). Cf. pp. 204–7.

Kremer, T. "The Significance of Solipsism," *Proceedings of the Aristotelian Society,* LX (1959–1960).

Kultgen, J. H. Abstract of "Can There Be a Public Language?" *Journal of Philosophy,* LXIII (Oct. 13, 1966). Read at the meeting of the American Philosophical Association, Eastern Division, Dec., 1966.

Lean, M. E. "Mr. Gasking on Avowals" (symposium), in R. J. Butler, ed., *Analytical Philosophy.* First Series. New York: Barnes and Noble, 1962.

Linsky, L. "Wittgenstein on Language and Some Problems of Philosophy," *Journal of Philosophy,* LIV (May 9, 1957).

Locke, D. "The Privacy of Pains," *Analysis,* XXIV (March, 1964).

Locke, J. *An Essay Concerning Human Understanding.* A. C. Fraser, ed., 2 vols. New York: Dover Publications, Inc., 1959. Esp. Bk. III.

Long, D. C. "The Philosophical Concept of a Human Body," *Philosophical Review,* LXXIII (July, 1964).

Long, T. A. "The Problem of Pain and Contextual Implication," *Philosophy and Phenomenological Research,* XXVI (Sept., 1965).

———. "Strawson and the Pains of Others," *Australasian Journal of Philosophy,* XLIII (May, 1965).

Louch, A. R. "Privileged Access," *Mind*, LXXIV (April, 1965).

Mackie, J. L. "Are There Any Incorrigible Empirical Statements?" *Australasian Journal of Philosophy*, XLI (May, 1963).

Malcolm, N. "Behaviorism as a Philosophy of Psychology," in T. W. Wann, ed., *Behaviorism and Phenomenology: Contrasting Bases for Modern Psychology.* Chicago: University of Chicago Press, 1964.

————. *Dreaming*. London: Routledge and Kegan Paul, 1959. Esp. Ch. XII.

————. "Dreaming and Skepticism," *Philosophical Review*, LXV (Jan., 1956). Cf. p. 23.

————. "Knowledge of Other Minds," repr., "with scarcely any change" (Preface), in Malcolm, *Knowledge and Certainty: Essays and Lectures.* Englewood Cliffs, N.J.: Prentice-Hall, Inc., 1963. Orig. in *Journal of Philosophy*, LV (Nov. 6, 1958).

————. *Ludwig Wittgenstein: A Memoir.* London: Oxford University Press, 1958. Cf. pp. 65–66, 87–92.

————. "Memory and the Past," repr. in Malcolm, *Knowledge and Certainty: Essays and Lectures.* Englewood Cliffs, N.J.: Prentice-Hall, Inc., 1963. Orig. in *Monist*, XLVII (Winter, 1963).

————. "The Privacy of Experience," in A. Stroll, ed., *Epistemology, New Essays in the Theory of Knowledge.* New York: Harper & Row, 1967.

————. "Professor Ayer on Dreaming," *Journal of Philosophy*, LVIII (May 25, 1961).

————. "Wittgenstein's *Philosophical Investigations*," repr.— "There is some correction of the text and there are new footnotes." (Preface)—in Malcolm, *Knowledge and Certainty: Essays and Lectures.* Englewood Cliffs, N.J.: Prentice-Hall, Inc., 1963. Orig. in *Philosophical Review*, LXIII (Oct., 1954).

————. "Wittgenstein's *Philosophische Bemerkungen*," *Philosophical Review*, LXXVI (April, 1967). Esp. pp. 226–27.

Margolis, J. "The Privacy of Sensations," *Ratio*, VI (Dec., 1964).

————. "The Problem of Criteria of Pain," *Dialogue*, IV (June, 1965).

Mayo, B. "Belief and Constraint," *Proceedings of the Aristotelian Society*, LXIV (1963–1964).

Medlin, B. "Critical Notice" of *The Concept of a Person and Other Essays* by A. J. Ayer, *Australasian Journal of Philosophy*, XLII (Dec., 1964).

Meiland, J. W. "Meaning, Identification and Other Minds," *Australasian Journal of Philosophy*, XLII (Dec., 1964).

Melden, A. I. *Free Action*. London: Routledge and Kegan Paul, 1961. Esp. pp. 33–37, 47, 53, 167–70.

Mellor, W. W. "Three Problems about Other Minds," *Mind*, LXV (April, 1956).

Mill, J. S. *An Examination of Sir William Hamilton's Philosophy*. 6th ed. New York: Longmans, Green, and Co., Inc., 1889. Cf. pp. 243–44.

Moore, G. E. "Wittgenstein's Lectures in 1930–33," completely repr. in Moore, *Philosophical Papers*. London: George Allen and Unwin Ltd., 1959. Orig. in *Mind*, LXIII (Jan., 1954); LXIII (July, 1954); LXIV (Jan., 1955).

Morick, H. Abstract of "Logically Private Ownership and Epistemic Privilege: A Critique of Wittgenstein," *Journal of Philosophy*, LXIII (Oct. 13, 1966). Read at the meeting of the American Philosophical Association, Eastern Division, Dec., 1966.

Mundle, C. W. K. " 'Private Language' and Wittgenstein's Kind of Behaviorism," *Philosophical Quarterly*, XVI (Jan., 1966).

Narveson, A. H. "Evidential Necessity and Other Minds," *Mind*, LXXV (Jan., 1966).

Olscamp, P. J. "Wittgenstein's Refutation of Skepticism," *Philosophy and Phenomenological Research*, XXVI (Dec., 1965).

Pap, A., "Other Minds and the Principle of Verifiability," *Revue Internationale de Philosophie*, V, Fasc. 3–4, No. 17–18 (1951).

Passmore, J. *A Hundred Years of Philosophy*. London: Gerald Duckworth and Co. Ltd., 1957; 2nd ed., 1966.

———. *Philosophical Reasoning*. New York: Charles Scribner's Sons, 1961.

Pears, D. F. "Critical Study" of *Individuals* by P. F. Strawson, Pt. I, *Philosophical Quarterly*, XI (April, 1961).

Perkins, M. "Emotion and the Concept of Behavior," *American Philosophical Quarterly*, III (Oct., 1966).

———. "Two Arguments against a Private Language," *Journal of Philosophy*, LXII (Sept. 9, 1965).

Phillips, R. L. "Mr. Aune on Strawson," *Mind*, LXXIV (Oct., 1965).

Pitcher, G. *The Philosophy of Wittgenstein*. Englewood Cliffs, N.J.: Prentice-Hall, Inc., 1964. Esp. Ch. XII.

Plantinga, A. "Induction and Other Minds," *Review of Metaphysics*, XIX (March, 1966).

———. "Things and Persons," *Review of Metaphysics*, XIV (March, 1961). Esp. pp. 505–19.

Pole, D. *The Later Philosophy of Wittgenstein*. University of London: The Athlone Press, 1958.

Pollock, J. L. "Criteria and Our Knowledge of the Material World," *Philosophical Review*, LXXVI (Jan., 1967).

Price, H. H. "Our Evidence for the Existence of Other Minds," *Philosophy*, XIII (1938).

————. *Thinking and Experience*. Cambridge, Mass.: Harvard University Press, 1953. Esp. pp. 153–55, 225–26, 240–45, 328–29.

Prior, A. N. "Rejoinder to Prof. Lachs on Omniscience," *Philosophy*, XXXVIII (Oct., 1963).

Putnam, H. "Brains and Behavior," in R. J. Butler, ed., *Analytical Philosophy*. Second Series. Oxford: Basil Blackwell, 1965.

————. "Dreaming and 'Depth Grammar,' " in R. J. Butler, ed., *Analytical Philosophy*. First Series. New York: Barnes and Noble, Inc., 1962.

Quinton, A. M. "Contemporary British Philosophy," in D. J. O'Connor, ed., *A Critical History of Western Philosophy*. New York: Free Press of Glencoe, 1964. Esp. pp. 540–45.

————. "The Foundations of Knowledge," in B. Williams and A. Montefiori, eds., *British Analytical Philosophy*. London: Routledge and Kegan Paul, 1966.

Rhees, R. "Can There Be a Private Language?" (symposium), *Proceedings of the Aristotelian Society*, Suppl. XXVIII (1954).

————. "Critical Notice" of *Science versus Idealism* by Maurice Cornforth, *Mind*, LVI (Oct., 1947).

————. "Wittgenstein's Builders," *Proceedings of the Aristotelian Society*, LX (1959–1960).

Robinson, G. "Following and Formalization," *Mind*, LXXIII (Jan., 1964).

Rollins, C. D. "Contingent Privacy That Is Complete," *Philosophical Studies*, XIV (Dec., 1963).

————. "Personal Predicates," *Philosophical Quarterly*, X (Jan., 1960).

Rorty, R. "Mind-Body Identity, Privacy, and Categories," *Review of Metaphysics*, XIX (Sept., 1965). Esp. Secs. 5–7.

Rosthal, R. "Ascription of Mental Predicates," *Philosophical Studies*, XII (Jan.–Feb., 1961).

Russell, B. *The Philosophy of Logical Atomism*. Repr. in R. C. Marsh, ed., *Logic and Knowledge: Essays, 1901–1950*. London: George Allen and Unwin, 1956. Cf. Pt. II, p. 198; also repr. by Department of Philosophy, University of Minnesota. Orig. in *Monist*, XXVIII–XXIX (1918–1919).

Ryle, G. *The Concept of Mind*. London: Hutchinson and Co., 1949.

Saunders, J. T. "Skepticism and Memory," *Philosophical Review*, LXXII (Oct., 1963).

Schlick, M. "Form and Content, an Introduction to Philosophical Thinking," three lectures delivered in the University of London in Nov., 1932; in *Gesammelte Aufsätze 1926–36*. Vienna: Gerold and Co., 1938. Esp. Pt. I.

———. "On the Relation between Psychological and Physical Concepts," in H. Feigl and W. Sellars, eds., *Readings in Philosophical Analysis*. W. Sellars, trans. New York: Appleton-Century-Crofts, Inc., 1949. Orig. in *Revue de Synthèse*, X (Avril–Octobre, 1935) under the title "De la relation entre les notions psychologiques et les notions physiques" and trans. from the German by J. Haendler.

Scriven, M. "The Logic of Criteria," *Journal of Philosophy*, LVI (Oct. 22, 1959).

———. "Views of Human Nature," in T. W. Wann, ed., *Behaviorism and Phenomenology: Contrasting Bases for Modern Psychology*. Chicago: University of Chicago Press, 1964. Cf. p. 179.

Sellars, W. "Empiricism and the Philosophy of Mind," in H. Feigl and M. Scriven, eds., *Minnesota Studies in the Philosophy of Science*, Vol. I. Minneapolis: University of Minnesota Press, 1956.

Shaffer, J. "Persons and Their Bodies," *Philosophical Review*, LXXV (Jan., 1966).

Shoemaker, S. "Personal Identity and Memory," *Journal of Philosophy*, LVI (Oct. 22, 1959).

———. Review of *The Philosophy of Wittgenstein* by G. Pitcher, *Journal of Philosophy*, LXIII (June 9, 1966).

———. *Self-Knowledge and Self-Identity*. Ithaca, N.Y.: Cornell University Press, 1963.

Siegler, F. A. "Comments" on Garver, "Wittgenstein on Criteria," in C. D. Rollins, ed., *Knowledge and Experience*. Pittsburgh: University of Pittsburgh Press, 1964.

Skinner, B. F. "The Operational Analysis of Psychological Terms," *Psychological Review*, LII (1945). Repr. in H. Feigl and M. Brodbeck, eds., *Readings in the Philosophy of Science*. New York: Appleton-Century-Crofts, Inc., 1953.

Slote, M. A. "Induction and Other Minds," *Review of Metaphysics*, XX (Dec., 1966).

Smart, J. J. C. "Sensations and Brain Processes," *Philosophical Review*, LXVIII (April, 1959). Repr., slightly revised, in V. C. Chappell, ed., *The Philosophy of Mind*. Englewood Cliffs, N.J.: Prentice-Hall, 1962.

Smythies, J. R. "A Note on the Fallacy of the 'Phenomenological Fallacy,'" *British Journal of Psychology*, XLVIII, Pt. 2 (May, 1957).

Stern, K. "Private Language and Skepticism," *Journal of Philosophy*, LX (Nov. 21, 1963).

Stocker, M. A. G. "Memory and the Private Language Argument," *Philosophical Quarterly,* XVI (Jan., 1966).

Strawson, P. F. *The Bounds of Sense.* London: Methuen and Co. Ltd., 1966.

———. "Critical Notice" of *Philosophical Investigations* by L. Wittgenstein, *Mind,* LXIII (Jan., 1954).

———. *Individuals: An Essay in Descriptive Metaphysics.* London: Methuen and Co. Ltd., 1959. Esp. Ch. I, pp. 40–44; Ch. III.

Stroud, B. "Wittgenstein and Logical Necessity," *Philosophical Review,* LXXIV (Oct., 1965).

Suresh. "Private Language and Sense Statements," *Philosophy and Phenomenological Research,* XXII (March, 1962).

Swinburne, R. G. "Privacy," *Analysis,* XXIV, Suppl. (Jan., 1964).

Tanburn, N. P. "Private Language Again," *Mind,* LXXII (Jan., 1963).

Taylor, D. M. "The Incommunicability of Content," *Mind,* LXXV (Oct., 1966).

Thomson, J. F. "Comments," on Castañeda, "The Private Language Argument," in C. D. Rollins, ed., *Knowledge and Experience.* Pittsburgh: University of Pittsburgh Press, 1964.

Thomson, J. J. "Comments on 'Wittgenstein and Private Language' by B. Gert." Paper read at the meeting of the American Philosophical Association, Eastern Division, Dec. 28, 1964.

———. "Private Languages," *American Philosophical Quarterly,* I (Jan., 1964).

Todd, W. "Private Languages," *Philosophical Quarterly,* XII (July, 1962).

Urmson, J. O. *Philosophical Analysis: Its Development Between the Two World Wars.* Oxford: Clarendon Press, 1956.

———. "Recognition," *Proceedings of the Aristotelian Society,* LVI (1955–1956).

Van de Vate, D., Jr. "Other Minds and the Uses of Language," *American Philosophical Quarterly,* III (July, 1966).

Waismann, F. *The Principles of Linguistic Philosophy.* R. Harré, ed. London: Macmillan and Co. Ltd., 1965. Esp. Ch. II, Sec. 4; Ch. III, Sec. 3; Ch. XII.

Watling, J. "Ayer on Other Minds," *Theoria,* XX (1954).

Weinberg, J. R. *An Examination of Logical Positivism.* London: Routledge and Kegan Paul, 1936. Cf. Ch. XI.

Wellman, C. "Our Criteria for Third-Person Psychological Sentences," *Journal of Philosophy,* LVIII (May 25, 1961).

———. "Wittgenstein and the Egocentric Predicament," *Mind*, LXVIII (April, 1959).

———. "Wittgenstein's Conception of a Criterion," *Philosophical Review*, LXXI (Oct., 1962).

Whitely, C. H. "Meaning and Ostensive Definition," *Mind*, LXV (July, 1956).

Williams, B. A. O. "Mr. Strawson on Individuals," *Philosophy*, XXXVI (Oct., 1961). Esp. pp. 327–32.

Winch, P. *The Idea of a Social Science*. London: Routledge and Kegan Paul, 1958. Cf. Ch. I, Sec. 6.

Wisdom, J. *Other Minds*. Oxford: Basil Blackwell, 1952.

———. *Philosophy and Psycho-Analysis*. Oxford: Basil Blackwell, 1957.

Wittgenstein, L. *The Blue and Brown Books*. Dictated 1933–1934 and 1934–1935 respectively. Oxford: Basil Blackwell, 1958.

———. *Philosophical Investigations*. G. E. M. Anscombe, trans. Oxford: Basil Blackwell, 1953. Esp. pp. 243ff.

———. *Remarks on the Foundations of Mathematics*. G. H. von Wright, R. Rhees, and G. E. M. Anscombe, eds. G. E. M. Anscombe, trans. Oxford: Basil Blackwell, 1956.

———. *Tractatus Logico-Philosophicus*. D. F. Pears and B. F. McGuinness, trans. London: Routledge and Kegan Paul, 1961.

Wolgast, E. H. "Wittgenstein and Criteria," *Inquiry*, VII (Winter, 1964).

Wollheim, R. "Privacy," *Proceedings of the Aristotelian Society*, LI (1950–1951).

Zemach, E. M. "Sensations, Raw Feels, and Other Minds," *Review of Metaphysics*, XX (Dec., 1966).

Ziff, P. "Comments" on Garver, "Wittgenstein on Criteria," in C. D. Rollins, ed., *Knowledge and Experience*. Pittsburgh: University of Pittsburgh Press, 1964.

INDEX